Liberal Parents,
Radical Children

By Midge Decter

THE LIBERATED WOMAN AND
  OTHER AMERICANS

THE NEW CHASTITY AND OTHER ARGUMENTS
  AGAINST WOMEN'S LIBERATION

 LIBERAL PARENTS, RADICAL CHILDREN

MIDGE DECTER

Liberal Parents Radical Children

Coward, McCann & Geoghegan, Inc.

New York

Excerpts from this book have appeared in edited versions in the January, 1975, issue of *Commentary* and the February, 1975, issue of *Atlantic Monthly*.

SBN: 698–10675–X

Library of Congress Catalog Card Number: 75–7529

Printed in the United States of America

To My Children—
Man the Lifeboats!

Contents

Liberal Parents,

Radical Children

ONE

A Letter

to the Young

My Dear Children:

I salute you this way despite the fact that as the world has always reckoned these things you are no longer entitled to be called children. Most of you are in your twenties by now, some perhaps even in your thirties. Some of you have children of your own. Yet you are still our children not only in terms of the technical definition of a generation but because we are still so far from having closed our parental accounts with you. We are still so far, that is, from having completed that *rite de passage* after which, having imparted to you the ways of our tribe, we feel free to invite you to join the company of its fully accredited adult members.

I am not so foolish as to suppose that you will be moved or even particularly beguiled by the idea that this book is most of all being addressed to you. For one thing, you do not in general appear to be very easily moved and certainly not very readily beguiled,or so anyway has been the experience of those of us who encounter you daily. For another thing, there have by now been so many books addressed to you, directly and indirectly—addressed to you, written for you, written by you, written about you: nothing in your after all rather brief lives, it seems, has gone unnoted, unrecorded, or unspoken. So you have no doubt, and with considerable justice, come more or less routinely to expect that you should be at the center of the concern of people like me.

I am a member of what must be called America's professional, or enlightened, liberal middle class. Though you were once taken to represent the whole of your age group, it is no longer a secret that perhaps the most celebrated youth in history—you, variously known as "our young people," "the kids," or simply "the young"—are none other than the offspring, both literally and figuratively, of this class. Not all of us, to be sure, are professionals. Some of us are businessmen, or the employees of businessmen, some the employees of government, and some ladies and gentlemen of leisure. Yet it is as certain that we are members of a common group—social critics have taken to calling us, usefully if not precisely, the "new class"—as that you are our children. You indeed, and our common property in you, are the primary means by which we make known our connection to one another. You all recognize this, of course, at least unconsciously (unconsciously is the only way most Americans in any case permit themselves to know what they truly know about class). Thus you would have little reason to take in any way but perfectly for granted my preoccupation with you.

Nor do I suppose that you will do much more than nod, hopefully politely, at the announcement that the book which is being addressed to you is not only about yourselves but in equal measure about the conduct of your par-

ents. You have long been in the habit of explaining yourselves by reference to your parents; in fact, you tend to
think about them and speak of them all the time—more
often, I think, and in a more intimate connection to your
own attitudes and behavior, than any young people before
you.

I will be presenting you here with a series of portraits of
significant types among you, as seen under the aspect of
certain of the patterns of conduct by which you have distinguished yourselves as a generation: dropping out of
school, using drugs, sleeping around, creating and defect-
ing from a communal way of life. These portraits are not
of real or particular individuals, though the experiences
ascribed to their heroes and heroines are, as I believe, real
experiences. As are the thoughts, ideas, and experiences
of their parents. If such a question is at all of importance
to you, it might be said that what I have undertaken to do
is an essay in fictionalized sociology.

Now, you would assuredly have your comforters, both
among your contemporaries and among mine, who would
absolve you of the need for paying serious attention to me.
"She is generalizing," they might say. "She speaks of no
one. She has no data, no studies, no documentation to bear
her out." This is the inevitable peril for anyone who seeks
to discuss the world through the medium of his or her own
senses. It is doubly the peril for anyone who seeks to say
that the evidence of his or her own senses is at odds with all
the things most piously and popularly being said. Still, I
ask you to consider: if the studies, the data, the expert
opinions had succeeded in illuminating what has been going on with you, our "young people," over the past decade
or so, why would we all feel—as we all undeniably do—that
there is still everything left to say? Why would what I have
called the pious and popular explanations of our condition

not long ago have satisfied our need to understand it? Why would we, in contemplation of ourselves, still be so indefatigably cheerless—you perhaps even more than I? I submit that the desperate desire of so many people to talk about themselves, to describe what they really feel—a desire for which the members of your generation have given possibly even more evidence than the members of mine—grows precisely out of a tacit acknowledgment that we have failed as a community, parents and children, to find a truthful and satisfying general description of ourselves. The solemn theories we have latched onto about you, whether they be political, ideological, or psychological theories, have not illuminated our problem. Nor have the voluminous accounts that you have so far given of yourselves.

I would caution you generally, in fact, about accepting any further counsel from those who would seek to absolve you of what might be considered difficult or unpleasant tasks, tempting as such counsel might be. Your would-be comforters, those who have so loudly and for so long professed to be your friends, have deceived you. They have deceived you not only about the nature of the world in which you have recently attained to adulthood but about their relation to you as well. Most of them have rushed to make a blanket allowance for you without even bothering to understand the nature of the behavior they have been so passionately intent on tolerating. In other words, they may have praised, but they have not really respected, you.

Take the case of your professors. They told you, they told themselves, they told the rest of us, that you were the brightest, most gifted generation they or the world had ever seen. We should have been delighted. Why, then, were we not? For we were not—not you, not we, and least of all those who made the claim. You were surely bright

18

and gifted—that was plain to see—but you seemed so infernally content to remain exactly as you were, so passive and resisting in the face of all the exciting possibility that the world around you ought to have represented to you. You were bright and gifted, but you were also taking yourselves out of school in numbers, and under circumstances, that first bewildered and then alarmed us.

The answer, we were told, was that you were too good to suffer all the uninspired, dreary, conventional impositions being made upon your minds and spirits. Your professors said that your indictment of your studies, and particularly of the institutions in which you were pursuing them, was a just one. It was your very wisdom, they proclaimed, which had brought you to make the indictment in the first place. Moreover, they hurried to abet you, those of you who managed to remain in school, in your demand to be taught only that which would reflect and deepen your own sense of yourselves.

Yet still you did not prosper—nor did we, nor did they. For as it happens, your indictment of your studies was *not* a just one. Nor could it have accounted for the malaise that you as students were suffering from. In any case, what your admiring professors did not tell you was that your attitude to the university was helping to reflect and deepen *their* sense of *them*selves. In your challenge to the value of their work they found the echo of some profound bad conscience, some need to be disburdened of an unfulfilled responsibility to you. Thus the comfort of their self-abasing tolerance was cold comfort indeed. And what in the end— one may well ask—did it avail you?

Or take another case, in some ways a more important and interesting one: that of all the journalists and critics and commentators who spent the better part of a decade discussing you. They told you, they told themselves, they

19

told the rest of us, that you were the most idealistic generation they or the world had ever seen. Everything about you, everything you did, was ascribed to an unprecedented new accession of idealistic zeal. You were the "constituency of conscience," no longer willing, like your corrupt and self-serving elders, to countenance injustice. Some of these critics and commentators said you were actually a new breed of people, the result of a strange and wonderful new stage in social evolution. You had come, they told us, to lead our society out of evil—the evil of a rampant, heedless materialism that was threatening to infect the whole world with a frenzied quest for ever and ever greater wealth, up to the point of extinguishing even life itself. You had come also—it was really the same mission—to bring peace. At any cost, it was said, you were determined to bring to an end the mindless violence, lust, and greed that had sickened Western society through the long centuries of its ascent into technological splendor and spiritual squalor.

You as the exemplars of this new selflessness, and we as your parents—not to mention the entire society that was about to be so redeemed—should have been deeply gratified: you, for the recognition of your high motives, rarely extended to those engaged in working a noble transformation, and we, for the simple fact that we had sired you. What we all felt, however, was not gratification but anxiety—a peculiar and unremitting sensation of distress. For if you were out to remake the world, you seemed on the other hand to be unsuited for its most rudimentary forms of challenge. You were hanging out in gangs, obedient to group consensus down to the last detail of dress and manner, on the basis of an agreement whose first principle was that neither the strength nor the duration of anyone's fellow feeling should be put to any sort of stringent test. Your

philosophy of existence called for a level of private demand coupled with a regimen of self-scrutiny and self-
expression such as, when acted upon, threatened fairly to
blot out the very materiality of others; and you were taking
yourselves off into rural or urban—or simply psychic—wil-
dernesses where you sometimes could not even literally be
found, let alone followed. And above all, you seemed to
find it difficult if not impossible to touch the world at just
those tangents where its real work was being done and its
real decisions being made.

The answer, we were told, was that you were too sensitive and caring, too much in tune with a higher order of
values, to allow yourselves to be dragged into the terms of
our brutish common existence. It was your very superiority, said the critics and commentators, your very refusal to
tolerate the cruelty and inhumanity of the acquisitive life
which had brought you to turn your backs on it. What the
pundits did not tell you was that their passionate advocacy
of your attitudes was the material with which they themselves were attempting to forge a powerful and well-paid
position in the world. Your hanging back from the contest,
in other words, had become the stuff of their own determined effort to win it. No wonder they beatified you: and
no wonder your anxiety persisted.

Finally, there was our deception, your parents' deception, of you, the most kindly meant but cruellest deception
of all. We told you, we told ourselves, and we told one
another, that the so-called new style of life you were in-
venting for yourselves was some kind of great adventure
in freedom. However we responded to it, whether with approval, anger, or anguished tears, we consented to call
your expression of attitude toward us and toward the
world we were offering you by the name of rebellion. You
were indeed speaking in the language of rebellion and

21

making certain of its gestures. But if you were, as you liked to put it, busily intent on "doing your own thing," you were also continuing to allow us to pay your bills. No matter how high or far you flew, beneath you always you and we together had seen to it that our parental net would be stretching—a financial net, a physical, and above all, an emotional one. The truth is that your freedom, your rebellion, even your new "life-styles" were based on a fiction, the kind of fiction that gets constructed between people who are, for their own separate reasons, engaged in denying the facts. We wrung our hands in the fictional pose of those abandoned, and continued to write out our checks and proffer the abundance of our homes and hands, no questions asked.

It may not have seemed to you that we were praising or comforting you, but there was great flattery in our treatment of you nonetheless, flattery of you and flattery of ourselves. We flattered you in agreeing to call every manifestation of disorderliness on your part, no matter how aimless or short-lived, a symptom of your stern rebelliousness; and we flattered ourselves with the notion that we were doing our very utmost to behave magnanimously.

Such, my dear children, was the admiration and encouragement of you that resounded through the American air of the 1960's. Who can be surprised that it has cheered you or benefited you so little? If there is any consolation to you in such a thought, it has cheered and benefited your parents even less.

Here we are, then. You are now full-grown, your lives becoming more and more fixed; and we have reached the point where it is no longer any use to deny to ourselves that we are middle-aged. And we are, all of us, left with a truly terrible need to understand why life became what it did for you.

It is of course a platitude lying heavy on the public tongue that people need to understand themselves and one another. We chant this platitude daily in our country, like a salute to the flag, and, I expect, are about as deeply touched by it. I say that the members of my generation need to understand what has happened to our children over the past decade, and that the members of your generation, if you are to make satisfactory lives for yourselves, need to understand it even more, and as I write the words, I can almost hear the cadences of boredom in which by now they march into the mind. How can I impress upon you—so impervious behind all your strategies of retreat and passive knowingness—the present urgency of the need I am referring to?

I invite you to look long and well into the faces of your mothers and fathers. You will see there the feigned control of people who have long been whistling in the dark and whose lips are now fixed in a pucker from behind which no further sound can issue. From one end of this country to the other, in each of the comfortable suburbs and fashionable neighborhoods that have been settled by the members of the "new class," are to be found people of my age huddling together from time to time in a great common bewilderment. What, finally, they are asking one another—and in the asking, creating the first basic vocabulary of an honest community language—has gone wrong with the children? No disputes, public or private, no ideological schisms interrupt the almost telepathic flow of gestures, signals, shrugs, sighs through which the parents of The Young are able to communicate to one another the harrowing tales of their disappointment and worry for the future.

Two women, barely acquainted, meet over some luncheon table. "How is your son X or your daughter Y?" one of them, in an ordinary effort at polite conversation, asks the other. With the reply, My son is in San Francisco, or perhaps it will be, My son is in Arizona, or My daughter has left school, or has returned to school, or has returned home and is thinking about what she might do—with whatever reply might be forthcoming, the two women will suddenly have come upon a common ground of empathy and interest. They may share nothing else, but between them now—with regard to what was once the most intimate but has become the most readily available of subjects—there has collected a whole unspoken but highly meaningful set of references. One of these women is telling the other what the other might, with only a minor adjustment of details, in turn be telling her: the children, having had every advantage pressed upon them, having suffered no hardship, beloved, encouraged, supported, sympathized with, heaped with largesse both of the pocketbook and of the spirit, the children yet cannot find themselves. The children are not, for some reason—may God please tell them what it is—in good shape.

A group of husbands and wives, old friends, spend an evening together. They have no need to ask one another the kind of polite questions asked by the women at lunch. On the contrary, they attempt to shut out the subject of children, for they have come together for a bit of fun. And in any case, they already know the answers. So-and-so's boy, he who once made his parents the envy of all the rest, handsome, healthy, gifted, well-mannered, winner of a scholarship to Harvard, languishes now in a hospital where the therapists feel that in another few months he might attempt a few simple tasks and ultimately—for the prognosis is good—even hold down a job, provided it is not of the sort to make him feel too challenged or tense. Another of the sons of this group has lately sent a postcard to his sister announcing that he has taken up photography and that as soon as he gets some work he plans to buy himself a piece of land and build himself a house on it. Yet another—his parents should, they know, be grateful by comparison with some others, and are frequently troubled with the realization that they do not feel so—is in business; he has organized some friends into a firm of handymen and movers and, rather to his astonishment and theirs, the firm is prospering. So-and-so's elder daughter is living, unmarried, with a divorced man and looking after his two adolescent children, while the younger has just set off in pursuit of her third—or is it her fourth?—postgraduate degree. Someone else's daughter, who lives at home, has taken and lost or abandoned five jobs within two years and now finds that she wishes to work only part-time so that she might paint. Still another, who is married and the mother of two small children, has discovered a marriage encounter group. She and her husband, she says, wish to broaden the range of their relationship, and they believe that everyone, including their parents, ought to do the same. One couple in this group have a son in Sweden, whence he exiled himself to avoid the draft. He writes to them weekly, demanding that they find some way to secure him an unconditional amnesty, for he wishes to return home; under no circumstances, he underscores, will he agree to submit himself to a term of compensatory public service. His younger brother has decided to give up farming in Vermont and enter law school. His parents, people of rather modest circumstances, are delighted to "lend" him the $15,000 that will enable him to devote himself to his studies and at the same time provide for his wife and young baby; they have mailed him the proceeds of the re-mortgage on their house and vacillate wildly between relief and the irrepressible gnawing fear that he may not, even yet, remain content. The sister of these two, a school-teacher, participant in a long series of painfully inconclusive love affairs, has taken to spending all her free time on various projects for raising her consciousness to a full perception of the injustices that have been wreaked upon her. She has grown surly, neglects her appearance, and is in an odd new way touchy and difficult to get along with.

As you know better than anyone, these are not extraordinary cases, these women at lunch, these couples gathered for an evening's recreation, unable *not* to talk about their children and at the same time wishing to use only the barest signals: X has left home, or variously X has returned home, sufficing by now to invoke a whole rich vocabulary of anxiety and bewilderment; X is looking for work or X has found work or X is returning to school or X has gone to Europe or India or Israel sufficing by now to speak volumes, nay entire bookshelves, of incomprehension at the turn things have taken. You know better than anyone, of course, that such gatherings and exchanges are taking place from one end of this country to another, from Los Angeles to St. Louis to Minneapolis, Cleveland, Boston, Washington, and by all means New Jersey, Connecticut, and New York. For they are taking place in the homes and communities in which you have grown up, and they are taking place about you, or at least about a good many of the people you know.

Fundamentally, the question your parents have not dared address in so many words, either to themselves or to their friends—and yet cannot any longer keep hidden behind some false front of approving good cheer or resigned hopes for the future—is the question that must surely, at two o'clock in the morning, be growing upon some of you as well. It is, Why have you, the children, found it so hard to take your rightful place in the world? Just that. Why have your parents' hopes for you come to seem so impossible of attainment?

Some of their expectations were, to be sure, exalted indeed. As children of this peculiar enlightened class, you were expected one day to be manning a more than proportional share of the positions of power and prestige in this society: you were to be its executives, its professionals, its artists and intellectuals, among its business and political leaders, you were to think its influential thoughts, tend its major institutions, and reap its highest rewards. It was at least partly to this end that we brought you up, that we attended so assiduously to your education, that we saw to the cultivation of every last drop of your talents, that we gave you to believe there would be no let or hindrance to the forward, upward motion into which we had set you going from the day of your birth. I don't believe that this was actually a conscious intention for most of us. We did not—anyway, most of us did not for most of the time—tell ourselves of these expectations in so many words. Yet they were unmistakably what we had in mind.

But on the other hand, not all our expectations were of this nature. Beneath these throbbing ambitions were all the ordinary—if you will, mundane—hopes that all parents harbor for their children: that you would grow up, come into your own, and with all due happiness and high spirit carry forward the normal human business of mating, home-building, and reproducing—replacing us, in other words, in the eternal human cycle. And it is here that we find ourselves to be most uneasy both for you and about you.

Of course, you would see, or would claim to see, in this concern of ours for you merely another confirmation of the leading attitude of the youth culture: that we are incapable of perceiving and accepting you as you are. It has after all been a major assertion of the songs you sing, the books you read and write, the films you devour, that we are too bound up in our timid, sickly assumptions about life to open ourselves to the range of the new human possibility that you have engendered. And for a long time, as I have said, we ourselves tried to believe in your explanation for our feelings. We permitted ourselves to be soothed and distracted by the idea that we were in the presence of a revolution, that you were not, as you might have seemed, displaying an incapacity to get on with your lives in an orderly fashion but rather that you were creating a new kind of order alien to and superseding our own.

Were you dropping out of school or otherwise refusing the blandishments of prosperity, security, and privilege? That was because you were attempting to fulfill a need, quite murderously neglected by us and our society, to return to the sources of natural being. Did you appear, from our point of view at first quite mysteriously, to be turning your backs on the kind of striving for excellence in all things for which you had been so unstintingly and expensively brought up? That was because you were engaged in transcending the mean competitiveness to which everyone in America had mindlessly been made hostage and were moving on to a new plane of gentleness and fraternal feeling. Did you seem to be getting dangerously attached to the use of drugs? That was because you were seeking to intensify the quality of experience, because—unlike us, hypocritically engaged in our own use of alcohol and drugs to still the mind and deaden the emotions—you were daring to recover the passional and sensory world so long denied to Western man. Did your initiation into sex seem to us curiously uneventful and haphazard, without moment or weight? That was because you were freeing yourselves from our own crippling obsessions with sex and restoring the whole process to its proper, inconsequent, exuberant animal function.

Such were the things we told one another, and tried to tell ourselves, about you for a long time. They were popular things to say; to speak otherwise branded us not only as enemies of the young but as enemies of all things virtuous in the liberal culture of which the youth revolution had become a cornerstone. They were also, I have pointed out, self-flattering things to say, putting us as they did squarely on your side and as such, on the side of all things new, daring, and open to the future. Above all, however, these ideas about you protected us, if only temporarily, from the sense of failure that had come to stalk us by day and by night.

Well some of us may continue to say them to one another—though fewer every day—but none of us says them any longer to himself. And you? Some of you are still prone to go on as before declaiming your superiority to the meannesses and the hypocrisies of the achieving society, and your sensitive refusal to have a hand in its crushing of the human spirit (although those of you who speak this way are doing so less noisily than you once did). But what are you truly, in the privacy of genuine self-confrontation, saying to yourselves?

You are adults now—or should be—no longer in process of formation or unfolding, no longer *in potentia* but fully here. Thus there are things to be observed about your generation on which the count is already in, things that can no longer be denied by us and that are the real and hard ground from which you must now proceed.

You will surely think that I speak harshly—if not worse. Though you have made a great point of how you have experienced hostility from us, I do not in fact think that you are actually prepared for the possibility that any parent of yours might discuss your behavior in simple moral terms. In social terms, yes, and psychological ones, certainly—psychology has been the main medium of all our communications—but there has been little in the history of our relations over the past two or three decades to give rise to the idea that ordinary judgments of morality might one day be directed from our side to yours instead of the other way around.

As it happens, my purpose here is not to preach but to *describe.* Nor do I mean to describe you alone. I shall also be describing us. One need subscribe to no school of thought beyond that of the plainest common sense to be aware that the behavior of the members of my class and generation as parents has had the greatest bearing on your behavior as our children. Yet the things that we, all of us, stand on the brink of recognizing about your generation are inescapably entailed in moral questions.

The first thing to be observed about you, then, is that taken all together, you are more than usually incapable of facing, tolerating, or withstanding difficulty of any kind. From the time of your earliest childhood you have stood in a relation to the world that can only be characterized as a refusal to be tested. This refusal was announced, sometimes literally, sometimes cloaked in the assertions of a higher creativity, in your schools. It shaped your attitude to play, to sports, to sex, to the reading of difficult books and the clarification of difficult ideas, to the assumption of serious roles within your families and communities, and to the consideration of possibilities for your future. It lent enormous impact to your experience of drugs, whose greatest seduction for you lay in their power to create the sensation of well-being with little or no effort on your part. Later, when you were either in or out of college, this refusal took on all the convenient coloration of ideology. The idea that the system was evil, and engaged in an evil war, provided cover for a number of your far deeper impulses to retreat from, or to circumvent, the demand that you take on distasteful tasks—whether it be to endure a bit of necessary boredom, or to serve in the army, or to overcome the anxieties of normal ambition. The word most frequently on your lips, in the days when you were said to be mounting your relentless campaign against evil, was "hassle." To be hassled meant to be subjected to difficulty of, from your point of view, an incomprehensible as well as intolerable sort. And everything, you assured us over and over again, everything we had either to offer or to impose upon you was a "hassle."

In the city where I live, which is New York, there are certain interesting ways in which a number of you have latterly taken to making your living: you are pushcart vendors, taxi drivers, keepers of small neighborhood shops that deal in such commodities as dirty comic books and handmade candles, you are housepainters, housecleaners, and movers of furniture. Let us leave aside the larger social significance of this—in American history, at least, unprecedented—voluntary downward mobility. In purely personal terms, all these unexpected occupations of yours have one large feature in common: they are the work of private, and largely unregulated, entrepreneurs—full of their own kind of woe, you have no doubt learned, but free of all that patient overcoming and hard-won new attainment that attend the conquest of a professional career. And they are free, most of all, from any judgments that would be meaningful to *you* as judgments of success or failure. Customers may irritate, and unpaid bills oppress you, as they do any private entrepreneurs; but there hangs over you no shadow of the requirement that you measure, ever so minutely and carefully, the distance of your progression

31

from yesterday to today. In the pushcart —many-layered symbol!—is bodied forth the notion that you might, if sufficiently displeased, simply move on to some new stand.

The second thing to be observed about you is that you are, again taken as a whole, more than usually self-regarding. No one who has dealt with you, neither parent, nor teacher, nor political leader, nor even one of the countless panderers to or profiteers from your cyclonically shifting appetites, can have failed to notice the serenity—the sublime, unconscious, unblinking assurance—with which you accept their attentions to you. A thinker, or a book, with ideas to impart that you do not already understand and agree with is immediately dubbed "boring" or "irrelevant" and must immediately thereby forfeit all claims upon you. For some reason, it seems never to occur to you that a failure to comprehend, to appreciate, to grasp a subtlety not already present in your own considerations might be a failure of your own. (In this respect, you very closely resemble that middle-American philistine known to my generation as Babbitt, superiority to whom has been a prime tenet of your, as well as our, self-definition.) What is more important, no member of the so-called adult community appears to have been deemed by you too imposing, too intimidating, or merely too plain busy to be the recipient of those endless discourses upon yourselves by which you make known certain delicate daily calibrations of the state of your feeling. The thought that some attitude or experience of your own might be less formed, less distilled in the twin refineries of time and intellection, less valid, than those of your elders, even those of your elders whom you have elected to call master, seems never to have crossed your minds. Thus, the entire world of thought and art comes to you filtered through a single supreme category of judgment: has it succeeded, or has it failed, by your own

32

lights to move you? To use your own parlance for this category of judgment, does it or does it not "turn you on"? Anyone or anything that leaves you unsatisfied in the way of private, self-generating response is remanded to obscurity. On the other hand, anyone or anything that touches or confirms what you already think and feel, no matter how lacking in any other virtue, is automatically important. Do you find yourselves peculiarly touched, say, by the songs of Bob Dylan? Well, then, he is among the great poets of the ages. Do you have a taste for movies in which the sound track has assumed equal significance with the images? Well, then, the true art-form of the age has been discovered. Are you disinclined to do certain kinds of work? Well, then, the very nature and organization of society is due for a complete overhaul. In short, you, and only you, are the ultimate measure of all that you survey.

And the third thing to be observed about you—it is really in some sense a concomitant of the first two—is that you are more than usually dependent, more than usually lacking in the capacity to stand your ground without reference, whether positive or negative, to your parents. So many of your special claims on this society are claims not on the distribution of its power but on the extension of its tolerance; what you so frequently seem to demand is not that the established community make way for you but that it approve of you. Take the case of your conduct with respect to sex. You have, you say, created a revolution in sexual behavior, particularly adolescent sexual behavior. But this revolution is not something you have done, it is something you have requested your parents and schools and other parietal authorities to do for you. It is in the apartments that we have rented for you, in the dormitories that we have sexually integrated for you, and in the climate of toleration that we have surrounded you with that you have pursued, in all passive supplication, your alleged revolution.

Or to state the case in the obverse, take the fashions in dress and personal habit that were so recently rife among you. Being children of the aspiring middle and upper-middle class, you had been raised by your parents with the expectation that you would be well dressed, therefore you dressed yourselves in rags. (Indeed, a little-noted feature of your sartorial fashion is how often it has been a kind of half-grown version of the games of "dress-up" played by little children in their mommies' and daddies' cast-off finery.) You were raised with the expectation that you would be clean and healthy, after the privileged condition of the class into which you were born, therefore you cultivated the gaudiest show of slovenliness and the most unmistakable signs of sickliness. You were raised on the premise that you would be prompt and energetic and reasonably prudent, and mindful of your manners, therefore you compounded a group style based on nothing so much as a certain weary, breathless vagueness and incompetence—enriched by the display of a deep, albeit soft-spoken, disrespect for the sensibilities and concerns of others. That the key to this entire assertion of style lay in an exact reverse translation of what your parents had taken for granted on your behalf is only one mark of how necessary we were in all your efforts to define yourselves, with the main issue for you so obviously being not "what in my own mature opinion will be best for me?" but "what will *they* think or how will *they* feel in the face of this present conduct of mine?"

Another mark of how necessary we were to your self-definition—only apparently a contradictory one—is that withal, you were never so adamant, never so energetic, never so articulate as in your demands that we lend our as-

34

sent to it. Not for nothing did you call the collective products of your search for group style and group meaning by
the name of "the counterculture." For it was a search that
utterly depended on, and was positively defined by, that
which it opposed. We had little cause to wonder that sooner or later so many of you, having had one sort of fling or
another out there in the wide world, would return home to
us, either from time to time for a brief sojourn or for what
in some cases has seemed to have become by now a perma-
nent stay. Where but at home were you to find the true
nourishment for your illusory sense of adventure? In
overcoming us, it seems, has lain your major, perhaps
your only, possibility for tasting the joys of triumph.

In any case, whatever you are lately in a mood to say to
yourselves, it is such thoughts about you that inform and
focus our own new mood as parents. Yet surely if a whole
generation of our grown children have been left with such
a great deal to undo in themselves before they can take on
what we all know, deep down, to be the essential requirements of membership in the adult tribe—surely in such a
case no one's shortcomings and failures are better reflected than our own. If you have a low tolerance for difficulty,
that is because we were afflicted with a kind of cosmic hu-
bris which led us to imagine that we were bringing up children as all our ancestors on earth before us had not had
the wisdom or purity of heart to do. In the life we promised ourselves to give you there would be no pain we had
not the power to assuage, no heartache we had not come
upon the correct means to deal with, and no challenges
that could not be met voluntarily and full of joy. There can
have been no more arrant disrespecters of the past, of the
sorrows of the past and its accumulated wisdoms, than we
members of the enlightened liberal community. And in
nothing can our assurance of being superior to our own

parents—wiser, kinder, healthier of mind and outlook, cleverer, more perceptive, and in better control of the dark side of our natures—have played a more crucial role than in the theories and practices which we brought to the task of parenthood. So we imagined, and taught you to believe, that pain and heartache and fear were to be banished from your lives.

If you are self-regarding, this is because we refused to stand for ourselves, for both the propriety and hard-earned value of our own sense of life. Our contentions with you were based on appeal, not on authority. Believing you to be a new phenomenon among mankind—children raised exclusively on a principle of love, love unvaryingly acted out on our side and freely and voluntarily offered on yours—we enthroned you as such. We found our role more attractive this way, more suited to our self-image of enlightenment, and—though we would have died on the rack before confessing—far easier to play. In other words, we refused to assume, partly on ideological grounds but partly also, I think, on esthetic grounds, one of the central obligations of parenthood: to make ourselves the final authority on good and bad, right and wrong, and to take the consequences of what might turn out to be a lifelong battle. It might sound a paradoxical thing to say—for surely never has a generation of children occupied more sheer hours of parental time—but the truth is that we neglected you. We allowed you a charade of trivial freedoms in order to avoid making those impositions on you that are in the end both the training ground and proving ground for true independence. We pronounced you strong when you were still weak in order to avoid the struggles with you that would have fed your true strength. We proclaimed you sound when you were foolish in order to avoid taking part in the long, slow, slogging effort that is the only route to genuine maturity of mind and feeling. Thus, it was no small anomaly of your growing up that while you were the most indulged generation, you were also in many ways the most abandoned to your own meager devices by those into whose safekeeping you had been given.

But of all this I shall speak in detail in the portraits that follow, where I have tried to tell a few exemplary stories, stories about parents and children, which describe the transactions that went on between us. They are not "true" stories, in the sense of being about individuals known to me or interviewed by me or whose case studies have been presented to me. But they are, as I have said before and as I believe, true stories nonetheless.

TWO

The Dropout

The one thing about which everyone agreed was that he was a boy of considerable intellectual gifts. While, it must be said, his school record had not unvaryingly reflected this fact—he had once or twice, for instance, shown himself reluctant, or unable, to focus his mind properly upon certain of the processes of mathematics, and one year he had flatly denied all requests to put any of the results of his work down on paper—neither his teachers nor his parents nor anyone who encountered him had ever entertained the slightest doubt that he was a very bright boy indeed. In any sea of faces his was always among those which carried that special amiable look of comprehension. He responded easily to new academic stimuli. He was, when genuinely motivated to do so, capable of mastering the most advanced and complex of ideas. And though he tended to display some weakness in the area of what educational psychologists call "spatial relationships," his capacity to verbalize at a level well beyond the national average for his age more than made up for it.

For the most part, his abilities were fairly represented by his grades. The year of his refusal to submit written work left no lasting mark. It was chalked up to some peculiar psychic conflict that time and maturity had obviously settled, and was forgotten. Even in mathematics he usually managed to lift himself, under the application of a bit of pressure, to a position comfortably above mediocrity. So while his record was not without an occasional blemish, it was clearly distinguished enough to allay any and all possible concern for his future.

In addition to his attainments at school, he had a number of extracurricular interests as well, interests taken up with at least the warm support, and sometimes the active intervention, of his parents. At the age of six, he grew suddenly randy for the prehistoric, particularly prehistoric animals. He demanded to know everything there was to know about them, insisted on being read to on the subject every night at bedtime, and most Saturdays, when offered his choice of recreation, demanded to be taken by his mother or his father to the museum of natural history. At the age of eight he turned his now conveniently fluent mastery of cursive script to the uses of poetry. For months he filled every available scrap of paper—his father's memo pads, his mother's laundry lists, some stock left over from a discarded finger-painting set—with ruminations set off in blank verse. Each of these works was rescued by his mother from the chaos of his room or pockets and placed in a special file hidden at the bottom of one of her dresser drawers. At the age of eleven, he turned to the guitar, and astonished everyone with how quickly he was able to pick out enough chords to accompany the singing of his favorite songs. (Later he was to astonish them even more by showing himself able, completely uninstructed, to do the same thing on the piano.) In time the poetry came to be punctuated with sketches and stories, these latter, after the fashion of ordinarily vigorous boys, somewhat lurid in conception, but in his case executed always with a singular and, his parents felt, disarmingly precocious sensitivity. The guitar did not last long, his impulse to play it apparently smothered by his parents' urging—they never ceased to regret it—that he take lessons. It was quickly supplanted, however, by a number of things, each in turn, that marked him a person of both resource and curiosity: the breeding of untold generations of mice; the organization and production of "shows," put on in his living room at the rate of about once a fortnight and calling on whatever talent he could discover within the circle of his playmates; the collection of geologically interesting rocks; and several other somewhat more evanescent but equally enhancing projects.

Between the generally hopeful development of his potentialities at school and the encouragement of his cultural avocations at home, then, it was apparent from the start that he was slated to become a young man of more than common accomplishment. His mother and father, themselves both well educated and deeply respectful of the role of intelligence in human affairs, often looked at him with an emotion that hung somewhere between satisfaction and wonder. Subject as they were to all standard parental anxieties, stern and angry and resentful as they could naturally be in the face of his lapses and shortcomings, in their heart of hearts they were perpetually amazed by this son of theirs. They compared him with themselves at the same age and found in almost every instance that he was not only a great deal farther along than they had been in actual academic achievement but infinitely more in command of himself and the world around him, infinitely better informed and more intellectually dexterous.

His mother, for example, who had herself written poems as a child, had managed to produce only a child's dog-
gerel—neat four-line stanzas with laboriously conventional
rhyme-schemes—duly recited in heavy-footed cadence before gatherings of family friends and relatives. He, on the
other hand, seemed to be tossing off sheaf upon sheaf of
original verse, some of which contained the most startlingly pure and precise imagery, and simply leaving it behind
in the trail of his general debris. And his father, far from
having been an amateur zoologist or geologist or impre-
sario, had devoted a good deal of his own boyish leisure to
the Boy Scouts, hot in his pursuit of a growing collection of
merit badges. In other words, their son was—to use the
only fitting term for their feelings on the matter—superior
to them. The thought, when it became a thought, delighted them.

They were not sure how to account for the phenomenon. It did not appear to be a simple matter of the boy's
Intelligence Quotient, at least not by the way that most in-
substantial of all human properties had thus far lent itself
to measurement. In any case, they were not inclined to believe that anything so vulgarly fixed and determined as
one's IQ bore any but the crudest relation to true intelligence. Then there was a notion in circulation about the
new generation of children that the presence of television
in their lives had served vastly to increase both their
knowledge of and sense of engagement in the outside
world. But they dismissed this notion, for in their view if
television filled the eye and mind, it also dulled the eye and
mind most regrettably. For their part, they always tried, albeit with no very great success, to restrict severely the
amount of television their son was to be permitted to
watch.

Clearly he was receiving better schooling than they had.

They had both attended neighborhood elementary and secondary schools in the years before World War II, schools presided over by time-serving teachers most of whom were themselves of uncertain literacy and who were forced to operate within a system and with a curriculum of which it might be said that at the best no harm was done. Along the way they had now and then encountered some special personality who had helped to fan the flame of cultural aspiration. But for them it had not been until college that there had truly opened up that whole resplendent realm of good books and important ideas and serious work which their little boy already seemed to be at home in.

Since their day educators had come under the sway of the idea that the mind of a child must be accorded full respect. In some cases this idea had become a mere caricature, leading to the substitution of mudpies and building blocks for ABC's. In others, it had led to nothing new, being an idea that required more of teachers than perhaps the very ordinary run of teacher could give. On the whole, however, it had created a certain openness and venturesomeness in the classroom, a certain appreciation for individual differences, and a certain imaginativeness in the shaping of pedagogy. Children who, like their son, had wells beneath wells of creative energy were being helped, or at least allowed, to give it expression and were not being held in total confinement to some prejudged standard of what they ought to know or ought to be able to do. His parents supposed, therefore, that some amount of what might otherwise have seemed to be his precocity was a tribute to the way he was being taught.

Still, in the end it was to themselves they tended to give the greatest share of credit. They were not particularly smug people nor were they much given to parental self-gratulation. Nevertheless, plain common sense seemed to dictate that they look for the sources of his gift primarily at home. They had long since gone dead to the argument over which was the more telling influence in a child's life, environment or heredity. Being educated middle-class Americans, they leaned, almost by second nature, to the environmental side of this question. Certainly before they had children of their own, they would have been prepared to argue that circumstance was everything as far as child development was concerned. Now they were not so sure; some aspects of their son's character and personality had seemed to them to be revealed almost at the moment of his birth. And with regard to his talents, except for his gift for music (alas, never to be properly developed), they were able without any difficulty to find an approximate origin for each of these in themselves. But the entire problem of heredity versus environment was neither here nor there, for the qualities of mind with which they might have endowed the boy genetically and the atmosphere of the home they were making for him were quite inseparable. Had he been a dull child, or a child in any way psychically impaired, they would have been forced to think long and hard about these matters. As things stood, he happened to be exceedingly bright; and they could not help feeling, though they were delicate about saying so even to one another, that he had, so to speak, come to the right place.

Even his being so much more sophisticated than they at a comparable age made a certain simple sense. They had not, after all, had parents like themselves nor grown up in homes like theirs. The education they had managed to wrest for themselves in the face of the benign and pious incomprehension of their own parents had become for him an established stepping-stone from which to reach still further. They could not imagine his reaching to a place where they, like their parents, could not follow and so would be left behind to nurse some mysterious hurt. But they could imagine his attaining to wonders of ease and poise and self-possession of which they had by the limitations of their own early upbringing been forever deprived.

They could not only imagine such a thing—it was the major conscious intention of their parenthood. No spark of their children's curiosity, they vowed, would go untended, no question unanswered, no misunderstanding left to fester or to frighten. Nor would any expense, either of spirit or of money, be spared in the effort for him to realize his full potential. As it happened, by the time he was of school age they found themselves blessed with what would once have seemed to them a gigantic annual income. The father had forged ahead rapidly in his career and was being recompensed accordingly, in addition to which the mother had come into a small but most helpful income from a family trust. Thus, while they were still far from wealthy, money represented no impediment to their ambitions about doing the best for their boy. They liked to think, however, that even if their financial condition had been far less propitious they would somehow have found the means to place him in the position of special advantage to which his natural endowments entitled him. Ambitions like theirs, they felt, were far more a matter of values than of mere wherewithal. So while every expression of some new interest on his part occasioned an appropriate purchase, either of equipment or of access to the necessary congenial atmosphere, while he was impressively widely traveled for one so young, while they had been enabled to arrange for him to spend his time only with others equally fortunate in the supportive encouragements of parents, it was finally in their most intimate personal relations with him that they saw themselves providing the greatest impetus to his intellectual development.

They did not urge him to this development, for the pressures to achieve put upon them in their own childhoods had often had the opposite effect from that intended. The unenlightened, status-hungry way in which the bright members of their generation had been pressed to maximize, and then display, all their accomplishments had often left them feeling precisely timid and inadequate. They could now, from the vantage point of adulthood, make fun of the pressures they had endured, telling again and again funny stories which acknowledged that, in the naked anxiety and greed for their children to enhance the family honor, the parents of that earlier time had not known any better. But the experience of parental pressure to succeed had not, as everyone so painfully remembered, been much fun while it was happening.

They would not be like that, they had long ago decided, with their own children. To them, a well-formed mind was not an acquisition to be displayed with all the other acquisitions of one's life but rather a privilege to be cherished for what it gave one in the way of freedom and dignity; and children were not to be seen as mere extensions of the galloping hopes and demands of their parents but rather as human beings in their own right, entitled to grow and to develop in accordance with the way life had seen fit to endow them.

Thus they did not urge him or press him. They simply opened to him all their resources. From the time of his earliest infancy no new striving on his part had gone ignored. They understood the meaning and respected the importance of each of his seemingly trivial efforts to master his little world, and lent the full weight of this understanding and respect to his encouragement. During the day, his mother was constantly available to him, seeing to it not only that he should be fed and clothed, protected and comforted, but that his life should be an ever-rich and stimulating experience. She was a charming companion, an ingenious playmate, and an absolutely untiring interlocutor. In the evenings, some time was always set aside for play and conversation, for solving the problems and summing up the profits of the day. Never did he go to bed without being read to or sung to and above all chatted with about anything on his mind. His toys were carefully selected, each one carrying some hidden dimension of stimulation to his mind, his muscles, or his imagination. His books, too, were chosen with care, for a flow of words that would please and at the same time enlighten him and for illustrations that would heighten his esthetic appetite. There were dozens upon dozens of these books, heaped in the sort of profuse disarray around his room that made them seem, as indeed they were meant to be, indistinguishable from all the other paraphernalia of play.

The most important resource they opened to him, however, was simply their capacity to talk. They talked to him, or to one another in his presence, almost without letup. Sometimes the talk was urgently pointed, and they held him, either with the intensity of their tone and glances or actually with their hands, and admonished him to pay attention. Sometimes the talk was aimless and companionable, like a caress. They talked to distract him—or themselves—from the eruptions of an ugly childish temper. They talked to console him for hurt. They talked to refresh him from fatigue. They talked to discipline him. They played private family games which were games of speech. They spoke to him of their feelings and taught him to speak to them of his. He swam in a sea of words. They prided themselves on never talking down to him and on never dismissing his questions with the assertion that he was too young to have an answer. They patiently explained everything for which he sought an explanation, even finding his interruptions of their conversations with one another neither a nuisance nor an irritation but an opportunity to broaden his imagination about the life around him. As he grew older, and primitive curiosity blossomed into independent observation and opinion, he was made a full partner in their communications. No one was surprised, then, least of all his mother and his father, by his articulateness. On the other hand, no one could fail to be impressed by it, either.

If his parents did not for a moment believe his school was primarily responsible for his brightness—or indeed, that schools could ever have more than an incidental shaping effect upon it—they were nevertheless determined that he should have the best education available. Whatever the stimulations of his home, a child needed the kind of training that only a school could provide if he were in the end to have a properly shaped, properly informed mind. He needed the challenge of his peers. He needed the guidance of experts. And he needed the long, slow, painstaking discovery of his society's massive cultural tradition. Now, schools had the power to turn this process of discovery, as their schools had done, into a muddy obstacle course or to make it, as it should be, an exciting adventure. Having to slog through an obstacle course would not necessarily make a bright student dull, but it would hold him back, mire him in needless frustration, and perhaps turn him sour on the whole business forever. The last thing they could accept for their child was the prospect of his spending years and years under the tutelage of people who either would not know or would not care about how best to capitalize on his gifts.

It was fated, therefore, for him to attend a private school. His parents could afford it—they would in any case have given up just about anything else in order to afford it—and their sense of what was important could have allowed of no other possibility. The question, of course, did not end there, for once they had determined to exercise some control over the conditions under which he was to be educated, they were faced with the problem of choosing the school they felt would be best for him. The city in which they lived offered a fair range of choice, and so they were obligated to have a more or less precise idea about what they wanted. They certainly did not wish for him to be pressed into some standard mold of achievement; he was not a standard child, that was the reason for their preoccupation with his schooling in the first place. Nor, however, did they wish for him to be merely indulged as a child of privilege. The right school for him would be the school which struck exactly the right balance between striving and indulgence required by his particular personality.

The community to which they belonged, a community of similarly situated and like-minded young parents, had as a whole come to lavish a great deal of care and concern on the problem of its children's education. Whether or not they sent their children to private school, and in the end a significant number of them did, all of these young parents felt keenly the obligation to see to it that their youngsters suffered as little as possible from the constriction and waste and foolishness that had dogged their own school days. Indeed, when they gathered together at dinners or parties—or even in their chance daily encounters—they spoke of little else. They grew scholarly in the practices of various schools and in the theories behind them. They debated the advantages or disadvantages of this or that method of teaching, or the virtues or shortcomings of this or that teacher. They exchanged accounts of their experiences with the school question, and commiserated with one another on the difficulty of bringing this queston to a happy resolution. They were not above laughing at themselves, aware that the difficulty was of their own making: they could so easily have sent their children off to the neighborhood school, as their own parents had done, and let nature take its course. But the responsibility was one they had solemnly undertaken, and it was no lighter upon them for any inclination to poke a bit of fun at themselves. Having no choice would have been easier for them but after all they were dealing with years and years of a child's life and with the most delicate process of nurturing a child's mind and spirit. The problem of education held the community close together; sometimes it seemed the very basis for there being a community at all.

The boy's mother and father, as it may be imagined, were particularly zealous in their attentions to the problem. Their son was, they found, a somewhat temperamental child, made so by a rare and precious sensitivity: he simply saw too much and comprehended too much to be protected from his feelings as other children were. While they hoped his sensitivity would one day be controlled and harnessed to a creative purpose, they did not wish for it to be crushed or distorted beneath the burden of the wrong kind of demand upon him. It was difficult to know in advance how he would respond to any given environment. In fact, the boy was to have entered his third school—in the third grade—before his parents were to be satisfied that he was in the right hands. The first school to which they sent him, at the age of three, had proven too chaotic. His teachers' inclination to let the children conduct themselves pretty much as they wished had left him too much at the mercy of his peers. He grew fearful of his classmates' physical bullying and anxious about their unchecked and unmoderated expressions of judgment upon him. He was taken out during his second year there and put into a school famous for its calm and order. Later they recognized that they had overreacted and gone to the opposite, equally unsatisfactory, extreme. Whereas before he had been anxious, he now tended to be glum about school. He did his work well and was commended for it—he had in the meantime learned to read and do simple arithmetic—but seemed passive and uninterested. When he returned home each afternoon, he would not tell his mother what he had done or what had happened that day—he who was normally so voluble. He began to complain of vague illnesses, quite nakedly to the end that he be allowed to stay at home. His parents intensified their efforts to make life interesting for him outside of school with new books, records, and outings to museums, shows, and places of special interest. Finally, on hearing for the fourth or fifth time, in one of those conferences with his teacher that had come to supplant report cards in all enlightened schools, that he was such a lovely, well-behaved, and quiet boy, they resumed the search for a proper school. This time they were successful. He was to remain in this third institution through high school, and he was to prosper there. His parents felt well rewarded for having persevered. They had at last found a congenial group of authorities and teachers both willing and able to share with them some of the responsibility for their son's self-realization.

It would not have been easy for them to say how they knew almost immediately that this school would prove a fertile ground for their little boy. Perhaps their very difficulty in naming a reason had something to do with it. For if any single quality characterized the school, it was an easy flexibility. The school was not dedicated to a set idea about how to teach children so much as it was dedicated to the well-being of the individual children themselves. The headmaster and teachers gave off the sense that they would be willing to try anything—including holding classes in the treetops or underwater—if this would genuinely enhance the children's response to their studies. When it was suggested, for example, that there were a large number of children in the school with a somewhat erratic distribution of achievement, advanced well beyond their years in one subject and struggling behind in another, they rearranged the curriculum so that each student could study each subject at exactly his own level. Sometimes this resulted in classes whose members ranged in age from ten to sixteen. The system looked messy but was actually, the boy's parents believed, a supreme state of order. When it was suggested that the inevitable competition for grades was distracting the children from the real task at hand, which was to learn as much as they were able to learn, the authorities abolished grades, informing the children only that the work they had completed was either very good for people of their capabilities or was not up to the standard they should expect from themselves. When after a year of this system—which happened to coincide with the year of the boy's peculiar paralysis—the children complained that they found it too difficult to understand whether or not they had progressed, the school reinstituted grades as the lesser of two evils. When a group of boys requested that they be allowed to pursue some advanced projects in science, a special hour was set aside for them and a special teacher provided. Following on this precedent, a number of children with special interests put in their own requests, and all, within the power of the school to do so, were answered.

The boy himself had no occasion to request any such extra consideration, because the areas of work about which

54

he was particularly enthusiastic had always been given a heavy emphasis in the school. He wrote a great deal. He painted—with no notable talent for draftsmanship but with great flair and imaginativeness. He sang—again with no very notable gift of voice but with true musical feeling. And he acted. In addition to full-scale facilities for art and music, and a drama department which staged elaborate productions of classical and contemporary plays, the school had always had, and had always attached overriding importance to, both a weekly newspaper and a bimonthly literary magazine. Thus, while the actual academic program of the school was probably no more suited to the boy's particular gifts than many another—indeed, than any other—might be, he seemed to thrive on the knowledge that he could at any time be most specially and individually accounted for.

In any case, thrive he did. He was found almost always to be a valuable contributor to each of his classes. Feeling himself to be valued by the school community, he maintained good relations with the majority of his fellow students and with his faculty. And in the general atmosphere of encouragement and appreciation, his work was quite consistently of good quality. Sometimes, as with English and social studies and the lab sciences, it was outstanding.

As he matured into a reasonably stable, serious, and remarkably sophisticated student, around the time of his entry into high school, a new element crept subtly into the concern of his parents and the rhetoric of the school: the future. Before long, the boys and girls were to have become young men and women; it was necessary for them to think of college. Their parents began to speak of it with ever greater frequency, and so did their teachers.

Now, thinking about college for the boy and others like him—his own classmates and all his contemporaries in the

American middle class during the 1960's—meant only one thing. It meant thinking about which colleges they might apply to and which seemed likely to accept them. There was no question about whether or not they should go to college in the first place—for their generation, college education had become the first article of a kind of unwritten Bill of Rights. There was no question about whether they *could* go. College was no longer viewed as an option but as a necessity quite as natural as the need to have a roof over one's head: whatever the economic circumstances of any particular family—and for most members of the middle class they were by this time unprecedentedly favorable—it had come to be perfectly taken for granted that the means for providing a higher education for its young would be found. The only question was, how prestigious and excellent a higher education had the children, by their display of scholastic talent and record of scholastic achievement, earned entitlement to? The competition, as they knew and as they came to experience ever more keenly with the approach of high-school graduation, was murderous. For one thing, there were many of them. They were products of a decade-long postwar population explosion that had left people of their age elbowing one another for space in virtually all the relevant institutions of society, including their own households and very much including their schools. For another thing, the colleges and universities themselves had, under pressure of the idea that America needed larger and larger numbers of well-educated people, and under persuasion from the federal government, come to a wholly new feverish preoccupation with academic excellence. If it was inevitable that they should go to college, they had to do well indeed to get into a desirable one. Small wonder that parents and teachers should begin calling their attention to this issue very early.

THE DROPOUT

The boy's mother and father had naturally had their eye on the question of his college from the beginning. They had sent him to private school because they had thought him worthy of and in need of the careful, private intellectual nurture he would be granted there. But they had also sent him to private school because doing so had seemed the soundest guarantee that he would one day be able to take his place among the privileged few being educated in the half-dozen-or-so best Eastern colleges. They were not much given to speaking bluntly on matters of caste or status, finding it unpleasant and generally very vulgar to do so; still, they could not help being conscious that private schools had ever been convenient conduits to the most sought-after private colleges. Whether they believed that this was right or wrong, in the case of their own son their course of action had seemed to them singularly clear and, they were happy to believe, singularly just. They were after all pursuing no mere baubles of status. They dreamed of Harvard-Yale-Princeton for the boy in quite the same way, and for quite the same reason, that they had already expended enormous effort to give him the best possible elementary and secondary education. He was a gifted boy. He deserved that his gifts, of mind and imagination and personality, be given the fullest opportunity to develop. This would best be achieved in a college whose traditions had long favored an occupation with only those members of society who were in one way or another exceptional. Of what use would it have been to him to have been the son of people like them if such an opportunity were not, by any and all means within their grasp, made available?

Their son, without any apparent conscious resolve to do so, seemed happy to cooperate with them in this matter. In response to the oh-so-gentle but unmistakably pointed admonitions of his teachers and the unspoken but equally unmistakable longings of his parents, the boy set about his schoolwork with particular care and thoroughness. This—as it was only natural to expect—produced a most splendidly reassuring set of results. In the end, he was accepted by, and duly registered in, a small, reputable college whose students were widely admired and whose training had almost automatically become synonymous with the promise of great future success.

If it can in some sense be said that everything in his life had conspired to bring about this happy outcome, might it not also be said that everything in his life had contributed to his own personal preparation for it? While not noticeably boastful or arrogant in his demeanor, he was far from unaware of himself as a gifted young man. Being accepted by a college to which most of his friends had not even bothered applying on the grounds that they hadn't a prayer of getting in would by itself have constituted decisive evidence of his superiority, had any such evidence been wanting. But the very intelligence for which he was thus being rewarded had long ago supplied him with the realization that he was no ordinary person. His parents' pride in him, though restrained in its expression by the manners of a community that required one to wear one's excellence lightly, was something he could easily see. They may have thought it the better part of policy not to praise him overmuch, and certainly not to brag of his accomplishments to others, but their true feelings could not be hidden from the eye of his perceptions. And the nearly reverential respect of his teachers toward the products of his creative flow—though his teachers, too, gave their feelings only minimal covert expression for fear of hurting the pride of others—was something that had become so accustomed in his daily life as to have resembled the very air he breathed.

The careful, searching way in which his questions had always been answered, his doubts always considered, his opposition or resistance always debated with him, had given him to understand almost as a matter of instinct that he was someone of considerable power. People clearly found it impossible to turn him aside, or to ignore either his presence or his opinions. Nothing he had ever turned his hand to, for instance, were it ever so large or ever so small, had been regarded by his parents as insignificant. From the paintings that, duly processed and framed, hung prominently in his home, to the lengthy family discussions of his views on the state of the world, everything in which he saw fit to engage himself had been accorded the status of a phenomenon to be dealt with seriously. Nor had his teachers ever shown themselves quite so pleased as when they found him warming to the material they were presenting—or, on the other hand, quite so distressed as when he took the occasion to question its value. Anything that failed to move him—a book, for instance, that they had assigned him to read or an idea that they were asking him to consider—immediately became doubtful in their eyes as a useful educative tool. Anything that did move him was on that count alone seen to be vindicated.

He had been confirmed in a number of more concrete ways as well. Seldom, for instance, had there been a school dramatic production of any kind in which he had not occupied a leading role, and seldom had he occupied such a role without someone's offering the suggestion that perhaps his future lay in the theater. He did not in fact dream of a future in the theater but absorbed the compliment within a broader general sense of competence and well-being. His literary works—in high school he had added criticism and, as he thought of them, Kafkaesque novellas to his poetry—were published copiously in the school magazine; and each time a new work appeared, someone, student or teacher, invoked the name of e e cummings. He had at some point retrieved his guitar from its dusty neglect and discovered that a new genre of performance he had devised for himself, half-spoken *pensées* on the pains of adolescence with a simple three-chord accompaniment, was much in demand at every social gathering he attended.

On the whole, however, his sense of himself was conditioned less by these specific successes than by a large and undifferentiated experience of his own essential value. He did not put such thoughts into words because to do so would have embarrassed him fearfully, but it had not—could not have—escaped his notice that whenever he stirred himself, people seemed to focus upon the fact, and whenever he talked, people seemed to listen. This was not a matter of arrogance or conceit; he was by temperament too affectionate and nervous to be associated with such qualities. It was rather the unavoidable conclusion of all the relations into which the outside world had ever entered with him. Two things he knew, as his parents had hoped and striven that he should one day do, without taking any conscious thought: the first was that he was important, and the second, that he was *interesting*, to those around him.

There was no reason for him to suppose, therefore, that his upcoming years in college would be anything other than merely the next episode of a continuing adventure in self-fulfillment. Naturally, he was somewhat uneasy at the prospect of being thrust into an unfamiliar society, of needing to make new friends, master a new set of mores, and so on; this, as he told himself, was only human. By and large, however, when the time came for him to leave home and set off for his new school he did so in the serene and sturdy conviction that what was about to happen to him was of a seamless piece with all that had gone before.

In its communications with him, the college had been most welcoming. He had been selected from among hundreds of candidates, a letter from the dean of admissions had said, because it was the judgment of all concerned that a young man of his interests and endowments would find the atmosphere and traditions of the college congenial and would have a valuable contribution to make to the life of its community. The school's very selection of him, then, seemed to him evidence that he had, as it were, been born and bred to go there. (He had, in truth, believed as much to begin with: though both relieved and delighted to receive word of his acceptance, he had not, in the final analysis, been at all surprised.) Moreover, since his main effort of the two or three years previous had been precisely to show himself qualified for such a college, he felt, academically speaking, already on the most intimate of terms with the place. He was ready, more than ready, for anything it had to offer. His teachers had said so; his test scores had said so; and the college itself had hastened to agree.

The scene of farewell with his parents was a somewhat intense one. His mother wept; his father, uncharacteristically silent, kept patting his shoulder; and he himself had a large lump in his throat. The emotions of the occasion and its participants were various, ranging from sadness at the passage of time to the pain of impending separation to the keenest of pleasure and anticipation. Each of these emotions was felt by all the participants in this scene in varying degrees. But the one emotion absent was fear. Neither he nor they had any but the sublimest confidence —so taken for granted, indeed, they were not even aware of feeling it—that he was on his way to yet a further series of successes.

How great must have been the shock, then, with which it

began to be borne in upon him somewhere during his first semester in college, that he was suffering from a serious case of disaffection. He was irritable a good deal of the time, and more than once found himself under the obligation to force back what might have become a fit of weeping. The smallest thing, a chance remark, a look, a gesture, would set him seething with resentment. Oddest of all, for the first time since early childhood he could not seem to get through most days without a lengthy nap—which, no matter what he said to himself about being exhausted, overworked, and so on, had soon revealed itself to him as nothing other than the need to get away, to shut out the world for a while. Whereas once upon a time each waking hour of his life had been a kind of sallying forth, now his whole life seemed only to be occupied with various strategies of retreat. His capacity to study had become fitful at best; and even fitful as they were, his bouts of setting out to accomplish his assignments were almost uniformly tedious and hateful to him. He disliked school, disliked his courses, his professors, and even his fellow students when they were in class with him. Try as he might—and he had, he assured himself, tried as hard as it was possible for him to do—he simply could not get his bearings.

He was at first hard put to give a name to his difficulty. It was certainly not, so far as he could tell, a social one. The dean of admissions had been right about one thing: the other students in the college had been immediately recognizable to him and were for the most part very much like him. His apprehensions about the need to find his way among a new group of contemporaries had been stilled soon after his arrival. Given both the size and social composition of the school, he had in almost no time found a number of classmates with whom he had a great deal in common and to whom he could, after only the most pre-

liminary kind of introduction, easily make himself understood. He had never been an especially gregarious young
man, being given to something less than saintly tolerance
toward a fairly wide number of human shortcomings. But
if not universally sociable, he did on the other hand have a
powerful impulse to intimacy. So he was by no means
friendless; and those friends he had were always privy to
the inmost secrets of his heart and mind and spirit. Often
his dormitory room was the scene of some late-night gathering in which smoke and music and private confession
mingled warmly in the air.

Nor, he knew, could his disaffection be chalked up to a
disappointment with his general surroundings. His earliest impression of the college as a physically pleasant and
comfortable spot—conveniently located with respect to a
metropolitan center and at the same time covered with the
leisurely expansiveness of the countryside—was proven
correct. He was afforded, and took immediate advantage
of, a more than ample choice of recreations, both urban
and rural.

But neither his new friends nor the various enjoyable
ways they found to spend time together seemed to affect
his basic and ever intensifying unease. For it was after all
upon being a student that his life was now centrally focused, and as a student, he was experiencing a strange and
totally unexpected malaise.

His classes, for instance, far from being stimulating to
his mind, left him at best bored and at worst with the sensation that he was gasping for air. Most of these classes,
like all the classes he had ever known, were organized
around the principle of student discussion and participation. Still, unlike any of the classes he had ever known, it
seemed to be a matter of indifference whether or not any
particular student actually took part in them. Anything he

himself said was politely, but usually no more than politely, received. He noticed that those who spoke a great deal were not necessarily more kindly regarded, either by their fellow students or by their teachers, than those who remained silent. Student views and responses seemed to be solicited not so much in themselves as for the service they might render in moving class conversation along one track and one track only. Objections to the nature or the quality of the material being covered were greeted at best with a tolerant smile. To put the problem in briefest compass, when he spoke he felt that no one was truly, genuinely listening. He quickly grew speechless and frequently consulted his wristwatch to ascertain how many minutes were left to the class period. He could not quite make sense of a system that demanded his presence and was at the same time capable of being so serenely indifferent to it.

He made even less sense of his professors. They were, to be sure, very different from one another. Some were witty, some dull, some, especially the younger ones, terribly earnest about making contact with their students, and some utterly distant, entering the classroom, depositing, as it were, their lesson for the day, and making haste to dematerialize into the thin air of higher and more heady concerns. Despite the variety in their rank and manner, however, they all seemed to share in a single odd, and to him unaccountable, notion about the nature of their transaction with students: namely, that they might demand much but were under no necessary obligation to give more than a strictly formal minimum in return. Even the young and earnest professors, who tended to sit on their desks, gesticulate a great deal in massive display of their intention to get some point across or die in the attempt, and translate their thoughts wherever possible into the current student argot, seemed to draw some invisible magical line beyond which the students might not cross. As it was to happen, during that first semester all of them were to prove themselves reasonably kindly and genial people; he would be able to summon no complaint against them—as some of his acquaintances were heard to do against certain of their professors—for being especially nasty or mean-spirited. True, too many of them appeared not to care in the least that they spoke incomprehensibly; one was, to his taste, unnecessarily brusque, evidently preferring being feared to being liked; one, his professor of composition, seemed to him an insensitive and desperately unfair marker of papers. None, however, could be accused of seeming positively bent on destroying him. But none either—there was the rub—seemed bent on *educating* him. He discovered that any complaint that he was having difficulty fulfilling an assignment brought little more than a shrug, and possibly a one- or two-day extension of the deadline, from even the best of them. Any expression of his lack of understanding of, or dismay with, the material being covered brought little more, no matter how kindly couched, than an admonition to carry on. It was the chosen lifework of these professors to bring him along; moreover, they were being paid to do so; yet they either refused to, or could not, help him to find any gratification in the performance of what they asked of him. He could not say what their commitment was exactly. Whatever it was, it was quite clearly fixed at some point beyond the welfare of their students.

But each one of these difficulties—the tedium of his classes, his inability to impress upon his professors the urgency of his needs and feelings—appeared to him only an aspect of a far larger and more traumatic problem. This was the question of the institution itself, and most specifically, the question of his place in it. When he was finally able to give a name to his new distressing condition, at the moment when bewilderment began to turn to rage, he saw that what lay beneath everything was the single general presumption on the part of the college that it did not exist for him but quite the other way around. All the unique qualities of his mind and sensibility, all the creative energy, the gift, the brightness—in other words, the very assets for which the college had seen fit to select him from among hundreds and thousands of competing applicants —were not in this place to be given some final liberating release, but on the contrary were to be harnessed to the college's own purposes and intentions for them.

He had glimpsed and then quickly forgotten this presumption during the process of registering for courses, when he was virtually ordered to enroll in certain classes and forbidden to enroll in certain others. He had at the time been too timid, too taken with everything new, too unsure of his ground, to understand that the school's system of requirements and prerequisites was merely the entering wedge of an assault upon his individuality. When he did come to understand it, the rest fell into place: the classes in which the contributions of students were so subtly pressured to move upon a single point not their own, the professors whose concern for rousing the interest and curiosity of their students could not be allowed to exceed their commitment to cover so-and-so much material. He was not being taught, was the way he finally put the proposition to himself, he was being *trained*. Like a seal. No wonder he had spent so much of his time in class yawning, in a bodily and spiritual quest for an ever greater infusion of oxygen.

His insight into the nature of his predicament was not to attain to such clarity until well into the end of the semester. He was, indeed, to be aided in reaching it by a group of off-campus acquaintances—ex-students, artists, hangers-on, and other assorted free spirits—with whom he found himself in the latter weeks of the term spending more and more time. Meanwhile, he struggled and grieved, panicked, underwent strange bouts of illness, and gave up the struggle.

He began, from a sheer inability to keep awake, to slip out of his classes early. Nor did it escape his notice that his sudden departures were very little remarked upon. Soon he was simply not going to class at all. He continued to go through the motions of study, telling himself and anyone who would listen that class attendance was hardly necessary if one could still read and write. He set out to collect notes for two term papers, doing research for an hour each on alternate afternoons. For his freshman composition course he copied over a number of things he had published in the high-school magazine and submitted them one by one to his professor by way of a friend, who promised to explain that he was ill but nevertheless wished to keep up with his work. This method continued until he received back, by way of the same friend, his first paper covered with red-penciled comments so thick and detailed that he was unable to read them and his second paper, across the top of which had simply been written: "This was *not* the assignment!" He felt bitter and relieved at the same time—and all the more consoled, so he said, for not wasting his time in such futile endeavor.

In fact, bitterness and relief were the main components of his feeling about the whole question of staying away from his classes. He heard not a word from anyone about his absence. Thus he was apparently not in any trouble, and so felt relieved; but he was just as apparently, he noted bitterly, not of the least importance to anyone. Where was the dean or professor whose responsibility it might have been to exhort him to carry on and to whom he might then have explained his bewilderment at an arrangement that was asking so much of him on the one hand and on the other seemed so little concerned with the problem of whether or not he might be able to perform as asked? He had many imaginary conversations with such an imaginary authority, conversations in which he over and over again voiced his protest against a policy of selecting young men and women on the basis of their gifts and then refusing them even a hint of the proper expression of these gifts. His ethereal interlocutor had no answer to make; no flesh-and-blood one ever put in an appearance.

His independent work on the term papers went on for only a week, after which he discovered that he had not quite put his finger on what either of them was supposed to be about. He put away his notes and vowed to return to them when, under pressure of needing to get the work done, he would be able to sort something out. With the independent study of his textbooks he went on, officially at least, for a while longer; but in the end he set them aside, too. Apart from speaking nothing either to his mind or his imagination, they were written in a language that became more and more of a private, inaccessible jargon with the turning of every page.

With the abandonment of his books, his days became a round of seeking out conversation and deepening his personal relationships. He moved from hangout to hangout, from lounge to lounge, talking with various groups who were assembled to while away an idle hour. He found those who would talk with him about poetry and those who—first to his astonishment and later, to his rapt fascination—spoke with an almost choked and stumbling seriousness about God, about religion, about philosophy. The country was at war, though not yet seriously enough to impinge directly and materially on the lives of students; but there was some general talk of politics. This latter didn't interest him very much: he had certain basic political principles which involved siding with the poor against the rich, blacks against their oppressors, and peace-lovers against war-makers, and these seemed to him to serve him very well. But now and then he experienced a flash of illumination in the company of those who talked politics— the illumination that somehow peace and justice and prosperity and creativity (his own as well as that of mankind) were all one and indivisible. He found the politicos personally somewhat too wrapped up in their own concerns and too unyielding for his taste, and when the alternative was offered, preferred to move into the orbit of the poets and philosophers. Sometimes he carried his guitar along with him on his peregrinations and, if asked to do so, would repeat the accompanied recitations which had earned him such kudos in years previous. Again, he was often blessed with enthusiastic audiences; more than once it was suggested to him by some onlooker that he ought to cut a record. Now at last, he felt, he had come upon his proper matrix. He reflected on the irony of the fact that not until he had cut himself loose from the everyday requirements of college had his true education been allowed to resume.

Odd things had begun to happen to him, however. Some mornings he would wake up thinking of his parents and would be seized with a queasiness so profound that he could not get out of bed. The queasiness did not abate for all that he was able, with a high degree of psychological sophistication, straightforwardly to diagnose its origin as guilt. His parents were not unaware of his disaffection toward college. He had made little effort, in their weekly phone conversations with him, to conceal his feelings, and if either of them had given the slightest hint of demurring, he had even grown rather querulous. Initially he complained to them of his professors, charging them with arrogance, indifference to their work, or plain incompetence. Later he shifted his complaint to his courses, claiming that they were on the one hand too elementary and on the other hand far too technical. Finally, his indictment took in the college in general and above all the illusion foisted on young men and women like himself that going to a school of this kind would serve to enrich and enlarge their minds. The encouragements and counsels of patience his parents offered in response—until, that is, they realized that such responses were insensitive on their part and learned to hold their peace—sent small tremors of rage coursing through him. Still, he had not yet actually told them just how far his alienation from the place had taken him. He meant after all, when the time came, to get through his papers and exams and acquit himself creditably. Thus the thought of his parents sometimes left him queasy. Once he had even taken himself off to the student health service for some medication. Usually he found relief in the application of a marijuana cigarette or two.

Another thing that happened as the semester wore on was that the company of his fellow students began to irritate him, even so pleasant a form of it as he had found in his wanderings, guitar in hand, through the cafeterias and student lounges and dormitory halls. Despite the fact that their engagement in their studies was not immediately visible to him as they spent time together, the students came to seem more and more obsessed with the trivia of schedules and assignments, more and more preoccupied with the opinions, powers, and conduct of their professors. He detected a kind of benightedness and pettiness in them that he had not noticed before. Mostly they seemed to him young and callow and, poetry and philosophy and politics notwithstanding, submissive in an altogether unattractive way. As he had once been subject to endless fits of yawning in his classes, he now felt the same airless oppression just being in the midst of those who had either come from, or would soon be making their way to, such classes. He could no longer focus on their conversation and winced, literally, at the heartiness of their salutations whenever he approached them. His dormitory, once the scene of night-long sociability, now became a kind of agony of tiptoed avoidance.

Perhaps the oddest experience of all, when it came about, was the ease and suddenness with which he reached a blinding new clarity about the real nature of his problem. With all his flailing about and groping after the meaning of the trauma that coming to college had worked on him, in the end it took him only a day or two to put together all the pieces and give a simple, honest name to his discomfiture. In the shock of his original discovery that college was not at all as he had imagined—that students were being made to conform to demands supposedly dictated by some arbitrary notion of subject matter, and that, moreover, nobody very much cared whether they acceded to these demands or not—he had failed to understand why this should be so. In truth, he had always suffered from a certain weakness in the area of comprehending the origin and purpose of institutions. Though he had done particularly well, for example, in all those high-school courses that came under the rubric of "social studies," he had more than once had to confess to himself that he did not truly grasp the significance of a number of social and political arrangements over which so much had consistently been made. He had learned of feudalism, despotism, capitalism, and the like, and could accurately describe the replacement of one by the other in the course of time; but he had not concretely—in, as he would have said, his "own gut"—imagined them as related to the living substance of a living human experience. His own inclination, buttressed to a great extent by the conversation at home, was toward explanations for things that were more psychical than institutional. He believed far more in the reality of forces in human affairs that went by such names as ego, aggression, repression, and guilt than in forces whose names ended in -ism. It had not at first occurred to him, therefore, to think of the school's disappointing performance as anything other than a result of the failure of those who ran and staffed it to accept or sympathize with the individual make-up of its gifted young students. In thinking of it this way, however, he had found it possible to believe that with enough manipulation and cynicism, one might outwit the place. One could pretend to be tailored to the operations of the college, mechanically fulfill its expectations, and privately keep one's own counsel; nothing, he told himself, would be simpler. He did not in himself wish to do this, such strategies would be destructive to his nature, but if necessary it might be done. Was it not after all this very kind of accommodation that had come to seem so repugnant to him in his fellow students?

So it was that he continued to debate the issue of his own feelings and conduct, until the day when the insufferability of his fellow students literally drove him off the campus and into the orbit of a new circle of friends. These he encountered in a nearby bar and grill, famous for its tolerance of nonpaying loiterers, hangout for the bohemian fringe appended to the outer perimeters of the college society. Here there was no need for a formal presentation of self; one simply arrived, and was taken in. He had turned up, as was usual for him, with his guitar in tow; but curiously, he was never to remove it from its case. In this place, one had no need to *do,* one simply was: to call oneself a composer, for instance, was, by the custom of this particular country, all that was necessary in order to *be* a composer; assertion was by common assent the full evidence of deed. In the passage of a single moment, his heart warmed to the place and to the people in it. They in turn warmed to him. Such was the social style prevailing that no more than the most casually issued invitation to sit down stood between the ritual of introduction and the exchange of an all-naked intimacy.

Here it was, then, in the company of a group to whose table he was to return each day thereafter, that his eyes were at last fully opened to the nature of his predicament. Among the group were a number of former students who had passed through experiences exactly like his own and a scattering of others who had been too wise to the world to become entrapped in the first place. Unlike him, these people had long both known and trembled before the power of institutions to impose upon the lives of the unsuspecting. They understood what he had to tell them of his troubles even before he found the words. They nodded and sighed and laughed in mutual recognition of all his responses to the college and stratagems for dealing with them. More than once he was on the point of tears of sheer gratitude.

He had not realized—it was something his new friends were to illuminate for him with an almost incredible generosity of care and attention—he had indeed never in his life realized how much of everything he had done and striven for had merely been bait to trap his soul into serving the needs of society. College education, they helped him to see, was little other than a mechanism for leading the young safely into the enclosed careers and orderly, humdrum lives needed to ensure the survival of American middle-class existence. Colleges were factories geared to the production of steady, solid, efficient, and loyal citizens, people willing to spend their lives engaged in the creation of new and ever greater wealth and content to accept whatever were the going rewards for a life so spent. His puzzlement in the face of all that seemingly pointless academic activity was the puzzlement of a genuinely creative spirit in its first serious contention with the forces bent on its extinction. His boredom in class had been no mere fortuity. It was built into the very nature of the process, intended as a kind of basic training for the boredom—boredom and obedience and scaling-down of expectation—yet to come. By the time he had learned to move in perfect rhythm with the empty measures of academicism, by the time he had learned to contain, and then disregard, and finally to be unaware of, his boredom, he would have become the ideal passive vessel of business or academic enterprise—he could in other words account himself to have been successfully "educated." He could then leave school, marry, acquire a mortgage, kids, a backbreaking burden of possessions, and spend the whole of his human substance of inching his way up the ladder of career, all the while priding himself that he had in some small measure helped to keep the country running.

These ideas became clearer and clearer to him in the course of a number of conversations held around one of the tables in the bar that seemed to have been permanently reserved by the little society in which he was now spending most of his time.

He was able to admit to himself that one of the elements in his almost chronic stomach upset had been fear—not only fear of what his parents might think or how they might feel but fear that he was destined after all to be a failure. He had been duped into believing that going to college represented a fulfillment, and had paid for his credulity by suspecting, in the darkest hours of the night of the soul, that something must be wrong with *him*. Whereas, he could now understand, the truth was that the whole business of going to college was only the last—no longer hidden—stage of a conspiracy to bring him under control. He had been unable to concentrate on his work not because he had entered some mysterious and unmanageable new phase of existence but because the work was not, and was not meant to be, something enhancing and interesting to him. It was meant rather to stifle his energy and break his spirit and lead him, all anxious and submissive, into the role of a grateful drone.

He had always supposed that he would one day have a career of some kind, though he had never imagined concretely just what it would be. Sometimes he thought of being a poet, sometimes an entertainer; once or twice he had even imagined himself a great and rich and mightily powerful tycoon. Lately he had come to feel, particularly in view of the sheer volume of psychic and emotional disturbance he could not avoid seeing when he looked around him, that he might wish to answer the call to "do something for people." But that he should put his gifts at the service of one of the world's accustomed means for getting and spending had never for a moment entered his mind. It appeared, however, that this was precisely what was being expected of him, that this—and not, as had been advertised to him, the achievement of some higher and more splendid state of consciousness—was what going to college was for. In other words, he was in the end to be offered no opportunity other than that of simply taking his place in the footsteps of his father. The very thought sent a chill through him. For his father, whatever his virtues, was certainly no inspiring example of the joys of pursuing a conventional career. It had not been lost on his son that he was a man whose life was restricted at every turn by conditions not of his own choosing. Though on the whole the parental tendency had been to whisper about such matters behind closed doors, even as a child the young man had been aware of how often his father's most important decisions had been influenced by considerations like money or what might either serve or hinder his worldly success. Frequently he had witnessed his father fretting, grumbling about his superiors, or—something the boy had for some reason found even more troubling—his subordinates, worrying about the opinion of others, or giving up his pleasures to the supposed exigencies of business. No matter how great an effort was made to conceal the fact behind a facade of energetic determination, it had always been perfectly clear that his father was a far from free and self-propelling man.

And now, as his friends by having themselves escaped such imposition had enabled him to recognize, he had all unsuspecting been set upon the same course. He had in other words been betrayed. His guilt and fear were replaced by fury, a sense of outrage so overwhelming that he could almost taste it—and the bitterness so thick it was almost sweet to him. Each afternoon he journeyed to the table in the bar and grill for a fresh application of outrage, and each night he returned to his room glowing with the protective warmth of the knowledge that he had been only a hairsbreadth away from mortal danger.

Curiously enough, his new illumination brought him no relief from the drowsiness and nausea that had been dogging him. If anything, indeed, they seemed to be growing worse. His morning recourse to marijuana no longer sufficed to lift him from his bed and into the world outside.

Even in the midst of the most diverting conversation with his friends, basking in the mutual exchange of admiration and confidences that constituted the essence of their relations together, he would find himself drifting to the edge of a discomfort much akin to seasickness. Thus, besides the balm to his soul, they began to offer him medicaments of a more immediate and practical kind: pills to rouse him and pills to soothe him. Taken in the proper combination, such pills produced in him a kind of steady, low-grade hint of well-being. Sometimes he grew careless or confused and took too much of one to be properly balanced by the other; once, for instance, he lay in motionless half-sleep completely around the clock, and once he slept not at all for two days. But on the whole he became quite proficient at holding off what was by now an almost constant promise of bodily illness.

Somehow—later he was to marvel at himself—he survived the first semester. His professors waived any scruples about his class attendance and allowed him to write his examinations. With the aid of an ever-helpful pharmacology, a couple of papers had been produced and a quick review of texts and borrowed notes had been undertaken. In one case, an obviously hopeless one, he managed to have a failure transformed on the record into an incomplete.

His parents, at least for the duration of his intersemester vacation, succeeded in silencing most of their shock at the sight of his grades. They were, for one thing, well aware that even for the brightest of young people college sometimes imposed an extremely difficult time of adjustment. Being on one's own, away from kith and kin, torn from the roots of habit and environment, could by itself be so profoundly upsetting as to leave very little resource of mind and spirit for the calm attention to work. To give vent to their disappointment that he had achieved something less than a brilliant success would only shake his confidence and add to his difficulty. For another thing, they had always been conscious of the degree to which their concern for the outward signals of their son's success was merely a hangover from the neurotic preoccupation which had been such poison to their own youth. If in their deepest instincts they were not, could not be, liberated from the issue of grades, in their minds and values they surely were. He would be all right, they assured themselves. After all, he was passing through the last and most painful stage of growing up. And something there was in the way he now handled himself—in the way he kept to himself, husbanded his privacy, in the new reserve, so careful it was almost sullen, with which he spoke to them—that indicated he had learned a great deal in these months away at school, albeit not perhaps in any way that yet showed up on his record. They must, then, be content to bide their time as he went through the arduous labors of finding himself. Had he been a duller boy or a more limited one, he might now be giving both them and himself an easier time, but they could not for one moment even dream of preferring that, could they?

So it was that he returned to school for his second semester with the not quite illusory idea that he was offering himself a second chance. Once registered in his courses—this time without a breath of resistance—and settled in his room, however, he could not imagine what had possessed him to go back. Familiarity had not softened the place but only made it all the more intolerable. He wandered around for two weeks in abject misery, withdrawn to the point where he found himself unable to muster the energy to seek out the company of even his nonstudent friends. Finally, with a burst of determination such as he had not experienced in months, he packed up, left a note for the dean saying he had quit, and set off for home. He was not sure what he would do; probably he would go to California. He had heard much of California in the past months; it had come to seem to him not so much a place as a condition, seldom far from the thoughts and aspirations of just about everyone he had recognized as a kindred spirit. In the meantime, he wanted just to sleep for days and days. He had never been so tired in his life.

When the dust was settled somewhat—the boy's accusations hurled, the father's rebuttals completed, the mother's tears shed—the parents realized that they were facing no less than the ultimate test of all their convictions. They had been granted the privilege of producing an extraordinary and gifted child. They had, moreover, understood, as their own parents had not and as the majority of the society all around them still did not, that to be gifted imposed on one a special set of needs and wants. These needs and wants had never been and could never be answered to in the normal conditions of the workaday middle-class world. A bright and sensitive person must in some sense always be an outcast. They, too, although perhaps much of the manifest surface of their lives betrayed no hint of the fact, were outcasts. Was it not this very detachment from ordinary values and conventions that had enabled them to create the atmosphere in which their son had so exquisitely flowered? For them now to respond to his decision to leave school with nothing but pained disapproval and dire forebodings would be a mark of their failure. They would be failing him, and above all, they would be failing themselves, turning their backs on just those standards of importance by which they had always tried so hard to live.

Were they to lecture him about the need to make a living, for example, they would be speaking with the tongues of cowards and hypocrites. Had they not managed to learn how empty, how bereft of love and valor and true satisfaction, was the mere compulsion to make a living? Were they to speak to him about that which extends beyond the making of a living, that is, about the possibility of worldly success, of making a name for oneself and attaining to the respect and admiration of the community, would they not be involved in a vulgar betrayal of everything they had as people of cultivation and sensibility learned to stand for? That such anxieties for his future were now setting a torch to their hearts only proved how much remained primitively imprinted on their nerves of all they had rejected in their higher beliefs. He had a right to seek his own way, a right granted him in the very nature of their relations to him. If what he sought to do seemed to them alien and frightening, that in itself was probably the evidence of his seriousness. One thing, they concluded, they would not do; one sin of an older generation was not to be visited upon any further generations but would come to an end with them: they would not reject him for refusing to live as they wanted him to.

They had always been much attached to him, but with the passage of time grew more and more reconciled to the idea that perhaps under the circumstances it was best for him to go to California. Though he had declared his intention to hitchhike, they bought him a plane ticket to San Francisco. At the airport, as he was about to go through the boarding gate, his father pressed several large bills into his hand and his mother issued a final entreaty that he write to them often.

THREE

The Pothead

Had they been the sort of people who knocked wood, or spit three times to ward off the evil eye, they might have done so regularly in contemplation of their daughter. She was such a sturdy, well-formed, robust and lively little girl. No parent could have failed to experience innumerable bursts of gratitude at having spawned a child as sound and healthy and pleasing to the eye as she. They had reason to bless their fate. Even in moments of grievance at some misconduct on her part—moments which in their case tended to become a bit overintense but which arrived no more often, they knew, than any sensible parents were well-advised to expect—they could not help being moved and beguiled by the sheer spectacle of her. Often in the midst of their sternest exhortations they would melt, and fall to smiling.

She was, for one thing, a creature in constant motion. Her company would perhaps have been rather dizzying and annoying to those who were out of touch with the ways of healthy young children, but it had to have been enchanting, indeed very nearly dazzling, to anyone who both understood and admired the capacity of properly endowed little ones to live in a kind of inner harmony with their own seemingly unending vitality. Seeing her at play—first in her crib, driven by that relentless unfocused energy which finds cessation only in sleep, and later, at the center of a magpie band of little companions, cavorting about with a velocity that could be exhausting merely to behold—it was easy for them to fancy that she was no less than an embodiment of that far-off and legendary state of grace before the Fall.

For another thing, she had about her always, in tears or rage no less than in a state of highest glee, an air of utter and complete well-being. They would have found it hard to say in just exactly what this air consisted. Partly it had to do with her color, which was high and glowing. Partly it had to do with her physical composition, with the limbs that seemed perfectly fashioned to do whatever, and exactly whatever, she wished or needed them to do, with the flesh that was at once both soft and firm, well-fed and at the same time well-used, with the unpracticed straightness of her spine and the unconscious easy carriage of her head upon neck and shoulders. Most of all, there was simply the expression of her face. It was clear from looking at her, as eyes or fingers or feet lighted on each new object of her attention, that no gratuitous or undue suffering—no pain not strictly necessary to the processes of growing up, no debilitation of protracted illness, and no accustomed injury to her *amour propre*—had cast a lingering shadow between her and the external world.

It must be said of her that she was not one of those starched and shiny little girls, scrubbed and powdery fresh and beribboned, who had once in times long before been the proudest displays of their mothers' earnest house-wifery. Her beauty as a specimen lay in something rather different from the solemn, pristine graces associated by tradition with the beauty of femininity. Not that she was in any way gross or bullish or clumsy, she was not. But if the truth were told, she was seldom completely clean—only, as her mother was fond of joking, in the bathtub itself. And if seldom without a smudge or sooty knees or a fresh stain somewhere on her clothing, she was even less often in a condition that would have passed muster on the issue of neatness. No amount of combing, brushing, tying, tuck-ing, it seemed, sufficed for more than a minute or two to defend her from the threat of impending dishevelment. Yet no one could have thought that the elegance of a well-tied bow or the crispness of a perfectly white shirtwaist or socks would in any way have enhanced her attractiveness. For it was not any dinginess of neglect which was com-municated by her tendency to come apart but rather the radiance of her lust for the world. She seemed to bear around with her the palpable evidence of all her curiosity and venturesomeness and pleasure in the savor of her physical powers. The very grit beneath her fingernails, re-moved as often as was feasible by her mother only to be instantly replaced, became a testimony to the extraor-dinarily vigorous condition of her body and spirits. Her parents called her "urchin," even on occasion in a less than fully admiring tone, but they would not have had her any other way.

In the end, of course, they did not knock wood, nor did they engage in any other like practices stemming out of ancient superstition. They were educated young Ameri-cans entering the second half of the twentieth century; they neither believed in the existence of an evil eye nor even that it might be taken as an occult metaphor for something real and abiding in human experience. These gestures of propitiation to powers beyond the rational or explicable, resorted to freely in the households of their own childhood memory, had once seemed to them merely foolish and laughable indulgences on the part of people who had not the strength of mind to concede that they in fact knew better. Now, as adults, having learned from the wisdoms of modern psychology how much there was in all such species of human conduct that come from a truly dark and primitive fear of life, the gestures of superstition seemed to them not only foolish but something far worse: namely, a refusal to accept the principle of cause and effect. To place the health of one's children into the realm of mere luck or good fortune was only the other side of the coin of resigning oneself to the advent of ill fortune—and ultimately, in that shady and unconscious way they had come so well to detect among their fellow humans, to a shirking of one's own role in the matter. Resignation of this kind had perhaps once served a necessary purpose in the lives of people who in their poverty or ignorance or backwardness had been helpless to make any effective intercession with the workings of a blind nature. Such an attitude, however, was certainly necessary no longer, and so it had come to seem to them not only unbecoming but downright suspect. Once, for example, when their little girl had contracted measles and one of the old crones among the family clan had insisted that they hang a clove of garlic around her neck, they found themselves quite disinclined to laugh, and had to recount the story to a number of different acquaintances before the general amusement had made a dent in their annoyance.

But though they refused, in thought as well as deed, to make obeisance to any invisible powers, they were far from ungrateful for the fact that they had been granted a sound and splendid child. If they confined their expressions of gratitude to the smiles with which they greeted her most mornings or to their tender glances when they slipped into her room at night to peek at her asleep, this was not because they were so arrogant as to believe themselves more worthy than the people who were forced to look upon their children with lacerated hearts. On the contrary. She humbled them. In the last few weeks before her birth, the mother had several times been seized by a premonition that her baby would arrive in some way mutilated, that it would be feebleminded, perhaps, or without some essential limb or organ. Later she would discover that such premonitions were very common among pregnant women. Still, knowing that it was a universal experience would in no way dispel the effect of her prepartum anxiety or the sense of relief with which she would, even months and months later, take note of the bouncing, vital being who had once occasioned that very particular form of maternal feeling. Her father, in his own way even more fearful because so much more detached from the process of her birth and early care and therefore often overcome with feelings of helplessness and incompetence, responded to her as to a reprieve. They did not fall upon their knees or utter hymns of thanksgiving, then, not only because they had no deity to whom they might sincerely thus address themselves but because her very robustness made the issue of her future welfare seem all the more serious a burden of responsibility upon them. Having been presented with a child the gods themselves, had there been any, would have smiled upon, they must prove equal to the task of being her proper earthly caretakers.

In any case, whether inclined to fall upon their knees or not, they could not help believing that their daughter, too, had been granted a special blessing. She was blessed to have been born where she was, and she was blessed above all to have been born *when* she was: so many were the benefits of simply being member of her society and generation. It meant, for instance, that she would avoid the ravages of a whole variety of diseases which had formerly been among the taken-for-granted hazards of childhood. And even of those diseases which remained, for which a preventive had not yet been or could not be found, the possibility of their leaving some lasting effect—on her vision, say, or her hearing or her heart or her complexion—had been vastly diminished. It meant that from earliest infancy on, she would be fed in strict accordance with the actual, proven needs of human nutrition. She would grow as tall and as strong, as pink and as bright, as it was within her full genetic potential to do. It meant that a number of those mysterious infant interferences with digestion and breathing, now recognized to be the difficulties of a tiny, untried system in adjusting itself to a vast and complicated new world, could be named and treated and relegated to their true insignificance. It meant that she would be clothed and shod and equipped so as to encourage rather than to inhibit the most enjoyable possible participation in life. It meant that should the need for it arise, no power of a highly accomplished medical and scientific community—to offer her relief from suffering, to heal an injury, strengthen or compensate for a weakness, or remove the source of an offense against her bodily peace—would be withheld from her.

Nor were medical and scientific benefits the only ones of this new age. For if her body had been born into a period in which it was to be spared all needless sapping and depradation, so also—so preeminently—had her spirit. Here too the arts of prevention and healing had been brought an amazingly long way in an amazingly short time. Some

88

of these arts were complex, involving delicate insights into the relations between emotion and behavior, and some of them were primitively simple. In essence, what they amounted to was that she was, in each distinctive stage of her development, to be allowed to be herself —without shame, without the cruel suppression of her wants and needs, and without alien imposition. She would be allowed to eat when she was hungry, sleep when she was sleepy, and take comfort when she was in need of comfort. She was to suffer no more forcible adjustment than was absolutely necessary to standards of continence and deferral that pressed her to a point beyond her individual capacity. She would, without the anguish of a long and unequal contest with authority, be allowed to be the best judge of her readiness for each new undertaking in self-discipline. She would give up wearing diapers, for instance, not at the point at which tradition had determined it was proper for her to do so, but when in fact command of her sphincters would seem to her both a natural and perfectly convenient achievement. Her use of fork and spoon and drinking cup, the pattern of her daily schedule of resting and wakefulness, her submission to the force of verbal request—the whole network of settlements and withholdings and accomplishments by which she was to prove herself an ever more fitting member of civilized society—would flow easily and without hurtful pressure from the rhythm of her own individual development.

These were not small matters to the psyche, her parents knew; for they had learned to be aware of how much petty crippling of the spirits, in themselves as well as in others of their acquaintance, how much pointless tension, how much loss of heart, how much failure of nerve, could in the end be traced back to ignorance and unwitting brutality with which such processes had been handled in their own childhoods. A cup, for instance, was not merely a cup; to a baby it represented the demand to relinquish the necessary and heartening consolations of suckling. The toilet was not merely an appliance for bodily cleanliness and social presentability; it was an instrument for negotiating the most delicate and complicated transactions of give and take, bestowal and acceptance. A scolding was not merely a kind of lesson in the definition of the permissible; it was a message about the larger issues of love and love's failure. Nothing in the life of a small child could, for those who had been granted a real understanding of that life, be regarded as only a small detail. Each parental ministration, no matter how routine or trivial in the adult scheme of things, carried with it, for the child, an extra shaping dimension of reassurance or denial. In the experience of denial, born of his parents' refusal to grant and to respect the workings of his actual nature, a child learned to look upon the universe as an inhospitable place. Such an experience might be buried deep, way below the level of daily consciousness, but it could never in later life be truly erased.

Moreover, the new spirit of acceptance would not be confined to issues of baby and child care only; it bespoke a far more general, wide-reaching desire to understand and acknowledge, and finally to offer a proper respect to, the demands and passions of youth as well. If they were ready to forgive their parents for the insensitivity that had left their generation with a lifelong legacy of unwarranted guilt and fear—and it could not in all psychological honesty be said that they were—they would in any case certainly not permit themselves, now that they had become the parents, to forget what lasting damage could be wrought in ignorance. Thus, in addition to the likelihood of a long and healthy life, their daughter was destined to enjoy the privilege of having come into a world prepared to accept her

on her own terms. Liberated from many of the possible
hindrances to her continued physical strength, she would
also be enabled, courtesy of the new wisdom about who
and what she really was, to grow up at the very peak of her
emotional strength.

They had vowed virtually from the moment of her conception that no effort on their part would be spared, no
stone left unturned, to guarantee her what had now been
recognized as the basic minimum necessities of childhood.
She had after all come into the world at their behest, and
they were after all the kind of people who had it within
both their intellectual and spiritual means to make her sojourn here a thing of joy. In her infancy they had become
veritable scholars in such fields as the condition of her
nervous system, the meaning and quality of her responses,
the structure and syntax of that whole language of gestures by which she made known her needs and her dis-
comfitures. In addition to the careful, searching attention
they gave these subjects at, so to speak, their original
source—spending hours together in the interpretation of
a particular mood or on the reading of a certain reflex
reaction—there were innumerable books on the ways of
infants and children to study. These books, the work of
experts, of doctors and psychologists and laboratory re-
searchers, described in detail just what parents might expect of their child at any given point in the child's growth
and offered further a goodly amount of exhortation about
how parents might best behave in the face of these expectations. The little girl's mother had read such books in a
somewhat wry spirit, finding them less the products of an
arcane research than compilations of the findings of simple common sense and thus quite obviously addressed to
women in rather shorter supply of this particular quality
of mind than she felt herself to be. But she read them nev-

ertheless and undertook with the backing of their authority both to inform and reassure her husband. For what they both felt very far from wry about was their passionate determination to commit no blunder against the well-being of their tiny and defenseless daughter.

Later, when the child had grown—could speak and make her way autonomously in the world—and they could take some measure of the results of all their striving, they were able to laugh a little at certain of the epic intensities of that first year. With the distance, and the full nights of sleep, and the easing of the awful sense of inexperience, made possible by the passage of time, they were able to see that one simple principle had lain behind everything she required of them and everything they had set out to do. This was the principle of sparing her any and all forms of needless discomfort. What they had been uniquely given to understand about children—the essence of their difference from all the armies of the unenlightened, past and present—was that a child's strength, of limb as well as mind, depended on the unshakable conviction that it was a welcome presence in the world. Now such a conviction was apt to be all too shakable in the experience of a very small person living in at best a vast and strange and frightening set of surroundings. Only a continuous stream of reassurances, communicated in attitude as much as in deed, could serve effectively to counterbalance a baby's sense of vulnerability before the onslaught of so much new sensation and so much unfamiliar circumstance. To permit—or even more important, to be oneself the occasion for—the baby's suffering one bit more than was clearly unavoidable was to dampen, perhaps permanently, the baby's feeling of security and mastery. The infant who demands to be fed and whose demand is promptly answered is given, with its food, the additional nourishment of knowing that it has been able successfully to exercise its power over a pliant and manageable universe. Whereas the infant who cries on unheeded, and ultimately gives up, is allowed to experience, along with its hunger, the first erosions of the spirit and courage that must always be the concomitants of failure. Discomfort, then, was not merely a pity to behold in the small and helpless; it could, if allowed to persist, contain a most damaging message of futility. Children who suffered more than they had to were likely to grow up weak and frightened, not to say impotently angry, for their earliest education in life would have been a lesson in utter powerlessness. The little girl's mother and father had, they could see, often been foolish, and even more often clumsy, in their treatment of her; but the specific details of their foolishness and clumsiness paled into insignificance beside their general loyalty to the notion that they must do everything possible to add to her feeling of security.

They themselves, of course, had been brought up by another principle entirely—if not, indeed, an exactly opposite one. The idea of parental duty in currency at the time of their birth had also been an idea about the need to build a child's strength. The strength in this case, however, had not been a strength of confidence in one's ability to command the world but something that went by the name of strength of character. According to this idea, it was a major feature of parental responsibility to fit the child out with a proper set of habits. The means for achieving this end was discipline, a discipline at first imposed from the outside and later internalized, so that the child would learn from the very outset to curb his demands and expectations, to suppress his more unamiable passions, and in all sorts of ways, big and small, learn to shape himself to the contours of society. It was essential that the child acquire

93

these habits from the very beginning, for children subject to early indulgence only experienced all the more shock later on, in their confrontation with society beyond their own family, and found they could not get along. Indulgence, in other words, weakened them for that future life in which thumbs might not be sucked, soiled diapers might no longer offer a carefree convenience, mothers and fathers might not be at hand to do one's bidding, tears and railings would be of no avail, and above all, in which each day would bring some new measure of the discovery that one might never on earth do or have precisely everything one wished. The infant who lay whimpering in its crib, learning to adjust the rhythm of its appetite to a fixed schedule, was believed to be learning a first and most important lesson in how to accommodate to the world. Just as the infant who cried itself to sleep every night, until the newly forming nervous system was able to record an instant association between lying prone and sleeping, was being taught to shore up a capacity for doing without that which could not and should not always be available. Eating, sleeping, keeping clean—these were matters of habit. To disturb the routine by which such habits were inculcated was not only to confuse but to undermine the character of the child.

So it was that they themselves had—no doubt whining and picking at themselves and in many other ways showing tendencies to be most childishly unprepossessing—been led to struggle their way through early life. It was, when they thought about it, small wonder that each of them in his and her own special way had been left with an impulse to settle for something less than all that the world had to offer them. Though they knew a considerable amount about the history of man's long and arduous journey from darkness into light, and though they understood that no new step could be taken into the domain of truth without a previous foothold in the land of error, it never ceased to astonish them that people could ever have looked upon the drama of the cradle and identified it with the problem of habit. The core of this drama was after all the battle of a vital, needy individual to claim a bit of ground and establish the right conditions in which to grow. That such a battle should at the very onset be layered over with notions of regularity, of order and control and resignation to the demands of the adult community, seemed to them not only cruel but ridiculous. How could a creature who has not yet eyes to see nor hands to grasp nor mind to comprehend, who was only a bundle of instincts and reflexes appended to an enormous, miraculous will to go on breathing, be made to "learn" anything? Instincts and needs denied were instincts and needs betrayed and soured, not trained. Nor, later, could this same creature, now turned little person, be taught to relinquish the need for suckling merely by snatching away the nipple or to gain control over the functions of bowel and bladder merely by being forced to spend an hour each day in a show of effort to do so.

No little sharpness and bad feeling had passed between parents and grandparents on this issue. Warnings to put the baby down lest she become spoiled, or to remove her thumb from her mouth lest she become habituated to it, solemn pronouncements that the time had come to introduce the baby to the toilet seat lest it become too late for her to accustom herself to it—all uttered with the weight of a senior authority that took itself quite calmly for granted—had occasioned, especially in the mother, a number of small wellings of rage. She had long since in her own life learned to isolate and downgrade the seizures of self-pity that attended memories of her early upbringing; she had even trained herself to turn them to the uses of comedy.

But where her child was concerned, any expression of the attitudes of that earlier generation had the effect of turning her to tigress. She suspected that what lay behind these attitudes was something more sinister than ignorance, something, in fact, more closely akin to revulsion at the nakedness of the human constitution which was revealed in the behavior of the very young.

In any case, she herself was aware of feeling no such revulsion; and had she detected any—some hangover, say, of an early conditioning—she would have been determined not to let it blacken her relations with her child.

But the course she and her husband had adopted was not an easy one. Far easier would have been to force the child to conform to their routines and habits—as their own parents were pleased to have done—and to look upon her difficulties in doing so as prime evidence that they were fulfilling their highest obligations to her. To offer her, as they were doing, the kind of full acceptance that would leave no crimp in her sense of security meant, for one thing, that they were to go a very long time without an entire night's quiet. It meant that each day would have to remain to some extent unplanned; that the routine chores of household, contacts with the world outside the nursery, meals, evenings of entertainment, would be slipped into the interstices of her demand. It meant above all that they would be called upon continually to hold themselves open, sensitive, to the questions of what she was feeling and how they ought to respond.

In her infancy and early childhood, this was a question to which they often feared they might prove inadequate— it took so long, sometimes, to determine what was bothering her. Once, for instance, it had taken them days and days of contending with a peculiar mood of fretfulness on her part before they had been able to determine that the number of her daily nursings had left her feeling short-changed in the matter of oral gratification. She made as if to devour first the nipple, then her thumb, and she fretted. They were able to bring her relief only after the mother, on a shopping tour of the drugstore, lighted on a small, 25-cent plastic contrivance called a pacifier, an ersatz nursing nipple to be hung by a ribbon around the baby's neck and used as the need or desire arose. The child was, from that day until some time around her third birthday, seldom seen without it.

Then, it had taken them nearly six months to discover that she didn't like the cleaning lady. The days on which the woman was around the house she was nearly inconsolable. Nothing they had learned to do to bring her comfort—rocking her in a rocking chair, holding her before a mirror, where she was so often diverted by the sight of her own antics, long warm baths in the midst of a whole fleet of floating toys, not even her pacifier—seemed to stop her nervous wailing. Until one day, in a kind of blazing intuition, the mother had seized upon the source of her daughter's disquiet and dismissed the woman. Afterward, she felt shaken to the roots by the knowledge of how blind she had been. There were other examples, not quite so significant; all of them added up to the fact that the mere willingness to offer a baby the full force of one's searching, respectful attention was often not enough: one also had to be imaginative, intelligent, empathetic.

The shock experienced by the little girl on first attending school had very nearly defeated them. She was four years old, and they had enrolled her in a nursery class which met each morning for just three hours. They knew that being thrust into a group of that kind where she would be only one of many just like her was bound to present her with the need to make a large adjustment. She had played long and happily with children of her own age already but never without the protection of her mother or father. They had questioned whether it was fair to throw her so early upon the impartial mercies of strangers and contemporaries but had come to the conclusion that the advantage to her in having so much more lavish facilities for developing her mind and body than they could provide would far outweigh any difficulties. They had not actually, however, been prepared for the violence and duration of her response. She had absolutely refused to allow her mother to leave her with the class. As long as her mother was around, she was quite content, and even cheerful, about participating in all the activities of the group; but the slightest hint—even a suspicious shifting of body on the hard little wooden stool in the classroom on which the mother had been consigned to sit each morning—that she might now be left to carry on alone, and the little girl lifted her protest to the very ear of heaven. For several weeks the mother went along, believing that sooner or later a morning would arrive when the child felt safe enough in this new society to let her leave. But such a morning did not arrive and, moreover, showed no promise of arriving. Finally, following on an agonized nightlong discussion between mother and father, an attempt to take a relative measure of the effect on the child's future sense of life if she remained on in the school or if she were taken out of it, they regretfully informed the teachers that they felt they had enlisted her in the larger social process too soon: she was not ready for it. She subsequently confirmed them in their decision, and rewarded them for it, by bouncing about the house in the sweetest of tempers for some time.

A year later she was enrolled in school, at the proper age, with little or no difficulty. They were grateful that

98

they had not persisted in their earlier error and thereby permanently poisoned the very thought of school for her. They did not like to praise themselves, but in a moment of utmost privacy, they did exchange congratulations that they had somehow found the wisdom to snatch so confirmed a victory from the jaws of so likely a defeat.

Not all their dealings with her, of course, partook of the qualities of triumph and defeat. Mostly they went through the days and the months and the years together in a routine, and if somewhat strenuous, also reasonably comfortable fashion. She was seldom ill, but there were a few unavoidable and minor bouts of disease—mumps, chicken pox, flu, a throat infection or two—and through these they brought her without the least impairment either to health or to spirits. They noted that she took confinement to bed very badly, usually requiring a constant supply of adult companionship, amusement, and distraction to keep her in the necessary restful state of quiet. When, after a lingering throat disorder, it was recommended that she have her tonsils taken out—she was by then eight or nine years old—they knew that she would find the discomfort and isolation of a hospital to be intolerable. The mother checked into the hospital with her, bearing a satchelful of toys and games and for two exhausting days and nights managed to save the child from the trauma that was lying in wait for her. Her difficulty as a patient, they concluded, was precisely a tribute to her high good health: she took pain and illness as a kind of affront, being really so unaccustomed to them, and responded by being outraged.

Other things affronted her as well. She could not endure being chided by mere acquaintances or strangers—a thing that threatened to happen to her somewhat more than was usual because the speed with which she moved about created the possibility for a goodly number of collisions, tippings, spillings, and stepping on toes. If she was present, the mother generally managed to sidetrack the threatened unpleasantness, interposing herself between her daughter and the putatively offended party. But if, as came more and more often to be the case as the girl grew older, she should be unjustly reproached by those with no proper tolerance for the ineluctable nature of children, the mother or the father would later be called upon to reassure her that such hostility was of no importance and no account.

She was frightened of sickrooms—again, they felt, because the accustomed realm of her existence was so much one of health and vigor—and they believed it best whenever possible to amnesty her from attendance in them. Obligatory visits to old and infirm relatives they remembered as one of the keener tortures of their own childhoods; they saw no reason, beyond an outworn piety which smacked suspiciously of a certain vengefulness against the tender sensibilities of the young, for such painful and after all bootless courtesies.

Once, when one of the child's grandparents had suffered a lengthy confinement after a rather serious operation, they had braved one of those drawn-out, tedious family grievances by releasing her from the need to accompany them on any of their regular visits to the convalescent. They could from the one side understand, and even regret, the hurt that this was bound to occasion, but from the other side, the side where their primary loyalty and duties lay, they were quite firm in their belief that the fear and disquiet that such a visit would cause within a child not yet equipped to deal with them were to no point and thus to be avoided.

Rarely, however, did the issues in her life come to so fine a boil. Generally they moved along from day to day, being raised and being settled within the natural patterns of the working family relations. One cardinal principle of the household was that she not be allowed to go to bed at night without some settlement, some reconciliation, of the day's ragged feelings. The thought that angers or hurts or resentments incurred in the daylight, either on their part or on hers, should be allowed to fester through a long night's dreaming was anathema to them. Perhaps sharpest of all their memories of childhood anguish were those banishments, unforgiven and unforgiving, to the dark. They often found themselves angrier with her over some petty misdemeanor than they had ever meant to be or imagined themselves capable of being. But at least, they said, she would not be forced to carry the burden of their irrational and excessive hostility long enough for it to accumulate and become unsheddable. Nor would they on their side be given the opportunity to cultivate small parental grievances into large ones. Many a healing hour, therefore, was spent in discussing the way they felt, the way she felt, the way all of them tended customarily to react to one another. They explained themselves to her and in turn nurtured her explanations of herself to them. Rarely was she permitted to fall to sleep with a carry-over of items and topics for the next day's emotional agenda.

That their policy had been absolutely successful in eliminating guilt from the spectrum of her unconscious life they would not have been so smug as to claim. Nevertheless, as the years wore on it became clearer and clearer to them that they were producing a child who was open and gentle to a degree that they, with their respective bundles of masked and thus indelible early passions, could never in a million years of self-discipline come near to attaining. Perhaps, they sometimes thought, too open and too gentle for the corrupt and wily old world into which they were sending her.

As her infant tendency to perpetual physical commotion

slackened and then disappeared into her advancing maturity, what they found buried beneath it was a personality vitally, almost tremulously, responsive to the currents of motion all around it—physical motion and psychological motion as well. She seemed to sense the presence of anything violent or untoward in the atmosphere around her even before it had been given the least expression; and on the other hand, she seemed to be aware well beyond the normal capacity of her years of what it was that she herself was feeling. They could not help supposing that this was a gift they had been instrumental in developing within her, having urged her at every moment to make known to them what was going through her mind and heart in order that she not be left with sinister imaginings about herself.

The onset of adolescence, then, produced in her an utterly naked expression of the turbulence through which both her soul and her body were being made to pass. Half the time she would appear before them in the guise of a provocative woman, painted, languorous, and knowing. She would patronize her parents, sigh contemptuously in response to any of their demurrers about her conduct or appearance, and waggle her hips in a manner meant to communicate to them that she was no longer to be excluded from the realms of worldly understanding. On these occasions her father would catch himself bridling, about what he could not say for sure, and her mother would attempt to interpose some soothing form of mediation. The other half of the time she would figuratively, and sometimes literally, pop a finger into her mouth and climb onto their laps, issuing an unspoken request that she be allowed for a while longer to remain in her carefree and so painfully vanishing Eden. Now it would be her mother who would show certain signs of tension and her father who would turn the scene into a form of family entertainment.

In either case, however, it would take them both only a moment of coming to themselves to recognize that they were confronting, in the purest and most undefended and healthiest of forms, that critical turning-point in human maturation. Gone forever was the rowdy little girl who had the power to delight them, no matter how she tried their nerves, by the mere spectacle of her animal well-being. Such well-being must now be put to other uses, expended in the struggle to climb the one last step into self-realization.

Here, they knew, was the ultimate test of their capacity truly to accept her. Precisely to the extent that that struggle into womanhood was made to seethe and bubble where it was bound to cause the most unease—that is, under their very noses—could they account it a genuinely successful one. Were they to die trying, they would not permit themselves to fail this, probably final, test. There was in any case no question of their dying, or anything like it; because if the seductress often made her father uncomfortable, and the infant, her mother, they were not so sunk in that old-time, gloomy resistance to life as not also to be vastly amused and fascinated by what they were being privileged to witness. For every clenching of her father's jaw, there were three shrugs of wonderment and illumination. For every sour taste in her mother's mouth, there were three smiles of recognition and tender empathy. It was the fashion among their friends to make jokes about whether or not they would prove able to survive their children's adolescence. Being sociable people, and generally humorous ones, they joined in the joking; but to one another they confessed their insincerity: they were not having a bad time, far from it. She was still, if one knew how to make the proper translation, a creature operating at the very top of her bent.

Thus they did not know whether to laugh or to cry, whether to offer her a kind of new respect or bundle her up in a warm blanket, on the night that she was brought home late from a party and deposited on the doorstep half-conscious, barely coherent, and violently ill. She was fourteen years old, in her first year of high school, and caught up in a perpetual round of informal late-night gatherings in the homes of friends and acquaintances and the acquaintances of acquaintances that were called "parties." From her condition, she appeared to them to have gotten herself quite seriously drunk. By her second hour of almost uninterrupted retching and vomiting, however, when she could neither be roused from her stupor nor put to sleep, they grew concerned about the fact that the alcohol seemed to be having an effect on her unlike the effect of all the gallons upon gallons of alcohol they had in decades of sophisticated living been called upon to deal with. She was, they thought, not merely drunken but very nearly hallucinating. Nor did disgorging the contents of her stomach bring her much of the expected relief. They began to walk, rather more carry, her around the house, and in a state that was a cross between defiance in the face of her humiliation and appeal to be put somehow out of her misery, she confessed to them what she had done. In the company of a number of friends she had been drinking cough syrup. Before the night was out she had finished off nearly two small bottles of the stuff and then had begged someone to bring her home because all of a sudden she had begun to feel herself on the point of death. A hurried phone consultation with the doctor assured them that as soon as it was feasible they ought simply to put her to bed and let her sleep it off.

Cough syrup! Vick's Romilar, she stumblingly told

them, was said to be among the most potent of the patent preparations, and she and her friends had on a dare sent the hostess' kid brother to the drugstore to bring them back half a dozen bottles. Once her parents' fear-inspired rage over the fact that she had made herself so ill was calmed by the sight of her deeply and peacefully asleep, they found themselves hovering somewhere between amazement and hilarity. They had forgotten, no doubt bedazzled by the knowingness of most of her conversations with them, just how ignorant and foolish it was in the nature of kids to be. They decided on a strategy for handling this situation with her the next day, and prepared a stern lecture. They would tell her that they perfectly understood and fully expected that she would at this time in her life be experimenting with all the possibilities for adult naughtiness, particularly with such glamorous and raffish forms of it as drinking. They themselves had not of course been immune to the temptations of grown-up wickedness when they were adolescents. But unlike them, she lived in a household prepared to look upon certain deviations from youthful purity without horror. If she wished to drink, she could and should do so in her own home and under the tutelage of those who could teach her how to drink properly.

Having prepared their lecture, and possibly under the sway of their feelings of relief that she was all right, they fell to giggling. Cough syrup, for Christ's sake! they kept saying over and over. She was adorable; she was impossible. Didn't she know better than that?

There, to be sure, was the rub. If they had on that night discovered that their daughter was now embarked for fair upon a course of teen-age exploration and posturing, they had been reminded, too, that from now on there would be

105

limits set upon their rights to journey with her. Now that she was growing up it was an important part of the respect owed to her selfhood that she take hold of more and more of the world on her own and that they have less and less direct guidance and protection to offer her. Among the aspects of the new humaneness with which they had committed themselves to treat her there had now to be an acknowledgment that there would be things she must for her own sake—for the sake of that very growth and health they had heretofore so carefully, and so fruitfully, been supervising—withhold from them. In other words, their commitment to understand her had to contain precisely an allowance for the possibility that they would sometimes be required to step back and forgo the effort to understand her. It would soon be the case, if it were not in fact already the case, that her calling upon them would cease to be a mere necessity of child-parent relations and would become, for them, a privilege they would have to earn—just as friends earned it, or even teachers—only after a display of equal, and mutual, human trust. They would be left to watch, to hope, and to pray for the kind of wisdom that would bring her, in time of need or difficulty—as it had the night before—home to them.

Looking back on all the history of their life as a family, they could not but feel assured that they would somehow always be able to find it. When at last they crawled into bed, they went directly and pleasantly to sleep.

Though her parents might have been rather conventionally conscious of her adolescence as a time of inner turbulence, to her it seemed on the whole a quite diverting new condition. She would not say she was never troubled. Every day, indeed, seemed to bring its predictable quota of unpleasantness—of quarrels with friends or small difficulties with school assignments or petty, and from her point of view quite baseless, disputes with her mother. And there was now, in an entirely new way, the question of boys: she found them exerting a power over her attentions that was suddenly quite disproportionate to the value received in her relations with them. Nevertheless, life had become interesting and amusing to her in an altogether new way as well. If friendship was something that required far more of her energies to manage than it had in the former days of ad hoc and changeable and essentially casual alliances, it had by the same token become far more intense and intimate. If her presence in school was introducing into her life new and disquieting demands having to do with something that her teachers kept lugubriously referring to as "the future," it was also providing her with a new sense of the opportunity to differentiate herself from others. Her shortcomings and weaknesses as a student had acquired an unprecedented importance, but so too had her own very particular talents. If her mother and she were discovering a whole area of minor differences between them that yet had the force to rouse them to a frequently mysterious pitch of anger, they were also now treating one another with an air of equality that was far from displeasing to her. In any confrontation between them, it was no longer certain who would be the victor, left magnanimously to accept the apologies, and understand the justifications, of the other.

Then there were the new freedoms, tributes to the acknowledgment of her advancing years. Her time, for example, had become almost entirely her own, to be spent without suggestion or supervision as she chose. She was mobile: transport, particularly the automobiles of her older friends, was accessible without the need to secure par-

ental compliance, as were all sorts of hitherto enjoined opportunities to make use of it. There was money in her
pocket—not an unlimited supply, to be sure, but for the
first time a real spendable amount—placed there out of respect both for her need for some discretionary power over
her expenditures and for her capacity, now, to exercise
this power responsibly. There were things she could do at
home, such as smoke cigarettes, which, while they might
occasion long and tedious expressions of disapproval,
could no longer be forbidden her. She was allowed to
dress entirely in accordance with her own taste and to entertain herself, within the boundaries imposed by the requirements of her health and welfare, entirely in accordance with her own preference. In general, to an extent
that she had never experienced before, her daily life had
been placed within the governance of her desires.

She was still, of course, far too young to be much given
to, or even much capable of, any sustained effort at self-
observation. But if the question of her temperament had
been forced upon her consciousness, she would have es-
timated herself to be a generally rather jolly person. She
had ceased to be the hoyden forever enshrined in family
legend, the center of a perpetual and, as she kept hearing,
fiercely noisy whirl of activity, but she certainly could not
think of herself or her friends as being in their new state of
maturity noticeably somber. They ran around a great deal,
albeit now with the aid of various artificial means of loco-
motion, they laughed a great deal, they played many
pranks, and they talked and chattered incessantly, either
face to face, or failing that, over the telephone. She had
many friends, and though all was not consistently sweetness and light among them—each day, it seemed, brought
some moment of tension or ruffled feeling between any
one of them and the rest—one of their most important
bonds of friendship was a common distaste for the prim-

ness and constricted ladylikeness of a number of their classmates. She could not call herself the leader of her circle, but it had not escaped her sense of herself that she was always included in the planning, and at the forefront of the execution, of any of their more rakish undertakings. When dares had to be taken, or intrepidity displayed for the encouragement of others, or silliness set off in order to rescue the collective mood, she was rarely to be found among the hangers-back.

She tended to be highly vulnerable to any show of malice, even if unwitting. Voices raised in anger against her (except her mother's) usually had the effect of turning her on her heel and speeding her from the scene. Any of her appeals for sympathy that went unheeded, or even worse, that were turned down, tended to ripen instantly into resentments that could not be concealed. On the other hand, no one was quicker than she to forgive when forgiveness was properly requested. She had learned a great deal about life from the intimacies she had been privileged to share, first with her parents and now even more significantly with her friends. There were fathers who were alcoholics and created unimaginable nights of squalor in the household. There were mothers so sick in their sexual attitudes that they hurled unspeakable accusations and demanded unspeakable promises. There were mothers and fathers, divorced and living apart, whose hatred for one another had become the constant obsessive theme of their relations with their children. She was aware far beyond the entitlement of her years of the things that could sometimes drive one's friends to be less than ideal companions; and while she was no less sensitive to their heedless cruelties, and no less offended by the idea that she should in any way be made to suffer for what were after all the crimes of others, she found it difficult to bear a grudge.

Thus, there was little in her experience to interfere with

the notion—it could not really be called a notion but rather a sensation—that both she and her life were full of the promise of good cheer. And whatever of this sensation had come to her through the ordinary run of her transactions with friends and schoolmates, it had certainly been a hundred times reinforced at home. How could she have failed to find an important truth about herself reflected in the pleasure and amusement that shone so often from her parents' eyes as they looked at her?

School itself, now that she had reached the age of thinking about it instead of merely accepting it as a given like eating and sleeping, she was finding a considerable bore. Where she excelled without effort, she found no interest, and where she did not excel, she found all effort to be more or less dreary. The school *day*, however, was frequently an adventure. First of all, there was the newfound fun, properly heightened by the fear of detection and reprisal, of testing the limits of the system. Cigarettes puffed in the corridors between classes while evading discovery by passing teachers; whole class periods spent unmissed and unnoticed in the bathroom; the carrying of impudence to a teacher to the last and highest point of the still unpunishable; forbidden forays during classtime outside the school environs for a cup of coffee or a bottle of Coke; the pinning up of obscene announcements—informed by a wit that sometimes seemed to her nothing short of brilliant—on the school bulletin board: all of these carried out in concert with some group of companions, and breeding, along with a delicious if in the end exaggerated sense of risk, the explosive joys of cameraderie. Beyond the testing of the system, there was also simply the adventure of society. There was play, there was gossip, at which she had become highly adept, and there was, finally, flirtation, no less absorbing for the fact that it bore the ever-present threat of small humiliations. On some odd mornings she dragged herself to school as if with weighted limbs. Now and then, on a plea of terrible fatigue or headache or menstrual discomfort, she did not take herself there at all. But most often she hurried off to school, unfed and all but uncombed and unbuttoned, as if under the press of the most important business.

And if such had become her existence in school, outside of school there was even more to beguile her. She was a passionate shopper, satisfied enough with the mere activity of browsing through department stores to be forever purchasing and returning, thus enjoying many dollars' worth of the fantasies of consumption for each dollar actually spent. Any hours that might otherwise have been empty could in this way always be filled. Though she had never fully recovered from her childhood of smudges and stains, and so was far from a perfectionist about her appearance, she had gained a new interest in herself. Lengthy periods spent before a mirror had yielded her many styles and shapes and shades of face, conformations of lips and eyebrows, coiffures, postures, and facial attitudes, each one the expression of a different persona or mood. Her desk, dresser, medicine cabinet became vast warehouses of lipsticks, makeups, tweezers, hairpins, rollers, and an array of other paraphernalia serving to make alterations, large and small, in her natural endowments. Most of this *materia cosmetica* was for her private edification only. With rare exception she presented herself to the world outside her own household fiercely and assertively naked of any artifice, as was the fashion of her generation, the drama of endless possibility being reserved almost exclusively for her communion with her mirror.

Secretly, illegally—largely through the good offices of a young man who lived down the street from her and had certain sly designs upon her person—she was learning to drive. Another young man with similar intentions, though he would forever remain too testily uncertain of himself to act upon them, was the leader of an impromptu semi-professional ensemble of musicians—two guitars, piano, and bass. Until a black rage over his inability to make a move in her direction caused him to turn upon her and bruise her soul with a number of grievous insults, he dangled before her the prospect of becoming the group's lead singer. (She sang not well but energetically, in imitation of a certain star performer whom she and her friends particularly admired.) Before the grim occasion on which the truth about her singing career was so violently brought home to her, she attended the group's rehearsals several times a week. Though she nursed the hurt of this experience for a long time—both the hurtful things that had been said to her and the revelation of the baseness of someone whom she had taken to be amiable and helpful—the time once occupied by rehearsals was nevertheless still taken up with music: virtually no afternoon or evening went by in which at least some amount of time was not spent in listening to, dancing to, or talking about the songs and singers of the moment. Nor did a day go by when she was not to be found talking on the phone for an hour or two, usually in some agitation or excitement over the nature of the information being communicated. So it was, whether to her joy or sorrow—and usually something of both—that her days and nights were perpetually filled.

And above all, there were the parties. They happened every weekend and sometimes during the week as well. These parties, which had begun to take place with the first budding of breasts, the first retirement of the girls from the softball fields and afterdinner streetcorner games, bore little resemblance, she thought with pride, to the sort of occasions that went by the same name in the imaginings of her parents. To the sort of parties that her parents spoke of, and themselves frequently gave, one was invited. One assumed a pretense, of dress and demeanor, that immediately marked the occasion off as a departure from real life. Usually the company was divided into couples, one female to one male, with the understanding that each member of a couple was in some extra measure responsible for the other. She herself had been to one or two such parties, given by the kind of pinched and proper girls that she and her friends were at certain pains to avoid, and had counted the minutes when she might be released from her phony social bondage. Their own parties simply happened. Word would go out that people were to gather on such and such a night at the home of so-and-so, and there, in kaleidoscopically shifting social groupings, on the prescribed night at the agreed-upon hour a rather large company would find itself gathered. The venue shifted from place to place, and with it, in imperceptible degrees, so did the composition of the group, but fundamentally it remained a single continuing party in installments. Nothing in the dress or air of the participants, except perhaps that they remained for several hours on end within the same four walls, was there to indicate that anything formal or celebratory was happening. Nor, but for the erotic gropings that punctuated the middle of the party but otherwise seemed to bear no relation to anyone's demeanor on arrival or departure, was the company in any way regularly or visibly divided into couples. Far from being a departure from it, these parties were for her the very essence of real life. They were like a foretaste of her elemental existence once the arbitrary impositions of schoolgoing and living as a dependent at home were lifted. They provided every sort of encounter she might wish for—human, sexual,

113

recreational—and, like life itself, some she might not wish for. They allowed her to test her reactions and open herself to the being of others without any of the perils to which such testing was subject when carried on under the eye of an alien judgment. They wafted her to a place and a condition in which she might be completely herself: noisy and bouncy and cheerful when she was feeling noisy and bouncy and cheerful, soft and reflective when she was feeling soft and reflective, and even sullenly isolated when she was feeling isolated.

The fancy that this was her real life, and the conclusion that she was fortunate in it, were very much confirmed by her parents. On those evenings when the group convened at her house, her mother and father beamed approvingly on everyone, shrugged little shrugs of self-deprecation at the music which blared from the stereo speakers, sighed with mock wonderment that had about it something of envy at the abandonment of the dancing, eavesdropped with deep fascination at the snatches of conversation that were to be overheard in corners and hallways and in the kitchen, and when the first overtures of erotic play were to be discerned from among all the gesturing, moving arms and legs, vanished from the scene with a conspiratorial wave. They were interested in her friends and made many comments of appreciation or admiration or sympathy. Her mother particularly tried to keep current with all the connections and doings of the group, following the elaborate twistings and turnings of relation with a keen sense of what each individual was like and what each was up to.

She became aware, mostly through her mother's expressions of curiosity, that there was something very special indeed in the way she and her friends conducted themselves. Life among adolescents, it seemed, had not always been thus. Once, the friendship of girls, her mother had told her by way of explaining her sense that children were now enjoying a telling measure of social progress, had been subject to the erosions of a fierce sexual rivalry; the friendship of boys had been conditioned by an almost unavoidable and sometimes murderous spirit of masculine competition; and the society of girls and boys together had been smothered beneath a burden of symbolic behavior —moves and countermoves more finely calibrated than a master's game of chess. These parties, in which no one appeared to be the pursuer and no one the pursued, no one the escort and no one the escorted, in which the coming together seemed to be as casual, and the being together as undriven, as such things are among mature friends who have chosen one another for genuine and simple human nourishment, bespoke a social and sexual ease which would in former days have been unthinkable. Even the erotic hanky-panky—here her mother grinned—had somehow been given its proper casual place within all the various modes of relationship.

But just the fact that she had a large number of friends and spent so much time gadding about with them was the thing that her parents appeared to approve most of all. Since the earliest days of her childhood she had noted their special pride and pleasure in the contemplation of her encirclement by a crowd of playmates. Not only her success but their success as well seemed to hinge on the degree to which any of her days was given over to laughter and motion. Solitude, silence, lassitude, any form of withdrawal from the company of her peers or from their company had been taken as a condition requiring an immediate remedy. Difficulty in school, for instance, had always been a matter over which they had counseled her to be patient and forbearing, to relax any anxious demands on herself; whereas unhappiness in personal relations, social difficulty with themselves or with others, had come first on the agenda of their nightly consultations over the years. If she was having a good time, in other words, they could not believe that they had reason to worry very deeply about any of the lesser difficulties she faced.

Thus, on the morning after the night on which she had made herself ill with the cough syrup nothing could have seemed more natural to her than that her parents should have responded to her little escapade as they did. They teased her a little, scolded her a little, reminisced for her benefit about some of their own juvenile high-jinks, admonished her, as they had planned to do, to confine these early experiments with inebriation to her own home, and took no pains to conceal from her either their amusement or their sentimental recognition that she was, alas, growing up.

She found herself a little startled, therefore, by the force of the anger that overtook her as she listened to them. The anger itself did not surprise her so much, for she had often of late found herself quite suddenly, and sometimes inexplicably, growing angry with them. But she was not prepared for the violence with which her blood began to course through her and rise into her skull. Her effort to conceal her feeling—after all, what opening had they provided for its expression?—left her drained.

The truth was, and they had forfeited their right to know it, this had not been her first experience with cough syrup. She had been dabbling in the use of patent medicines for some months. It had in fact become chief among the new entertainments with which she and her friends had sought to liven up the rather dull and backward company of some of their more timid classmates. And she had become quite adept at inducing in herself a state of easy, floating gaiety that made it possible to have a great deal of fun even when there was very little in the way of funning available to do.

What had happened to her the night before was that a certain unpleasantness with a former boyfriend—he had confronted her and made a number of giggling and contemptuous references to her past behavior—had put her entirely out of sorts. In this mood she had been resistant to any and all effects from the syrup save for ill ones on her brain and body. The more she sipped, the worse she felt, until finally, in a gesture of bootless defiance, she had placed herself directly in the line of vision of the offending young man and downed what remained in the last bottle. All of this bore no relation she could find to alcohol, or wickedness, or the aping of adults, which her parents had so ignorantly and patronizingly assumed. Alcohol made people aggressive and unreal, noisy, rowdy players in a charade of pleasure, able to loosen up only on the pretext that they were not being their normal selves. How anyone could imagine that this was a condition that would seem enviable to her, something to be aped, she would never understand—or forgive. Nor would she forgive the idea that she and her friends were so innocent of the world as to find great titillation merely in being naughty. With them, indeed, everything could be put exactly the other way around. They were looking for the opportunity to be not less, but more, themselves. The new possibility of fun that had come to them via pharmacology was not the possibility of naughtiness but on the contrary of a kind of purity of self.

She had long been trained to find out the contents of her heart and mind, had long understood—even before mastering the necessary language for describing the phenomenon—that communion with her own needs and desires and emotions was the surest path to healthy self-

117

possession. Under the influence of the tranquility she was now able to impose upon her spirits, she felt as if she were for the first time truly making her own acquaintance, and the process was soothing and energizing at the same time.

In getting high—a very different matter from the condition that went by the same name among the adults she knew who drank a lot of alcohol—she had learned how to appreciate and take pleasure in the smallest things about herself and her surroundings. During her very first experience of getting high, for instance, she had noticed the pattern of veins across her wrist and along the inside of her elbow, how like a river system they were, like one of the river systems she had been forced to occupy herself with in fourth grade, and she spent an hour delighting in the vision that she herself was thus a continent, or perhaps a whole universe. On another occasion she and two friends had spent an entire evening in recurring fits of hilarity over a single funny remark one of them had made. There was a time when the thought of an evening spent sitting in one place would have driven her to frenzies of planning and plotting and improvising some activity. Now even one square foot of space, or one line from a song going around and around and embroidering itself in a steady, even pattern, or a single new idea about herself, could be made the stuff of virtually a whole night's entertainment. With the right state of chemical balance, she now knew, any time could be a good time.

That she had failed to have a good time the night before was a mistake, a terrible mistake—the very mention of the words "cough syrup" brought a retching sensation to her throat—but it was not her fault. That her parents should have seized upon her humiliation as an occasion to instruct her, when in fact there were things in life about which she could now be instructing them, was the cause of her fury.

118

She felt slightly chilled, and had a headache, and spent the day in bed.

She had to admit, however, that her parents were not the only source of her discomfiture. Lying on her bed, moaning now and then with her discomfort of head and stomach, she finally gave conscious thought to something that had been brewing unconsciously within her for weeks. Her heightened appreciation of self and surroundings, it seemed, also had an obverse: and that was, that she was becoming ever more vulnerable to the power of those in her immediate environs to spoil it. The encounter with the young man which had turned the potentiality of pleasure into so rank a misery was only the most extreme example of the way in which many of her companions had lately done her down. Her voyages into new territories of the nervous system were proving to be a kind of acid test of the congeniality of those around her. And by that test, she now realized, a number of the people with whom she had customarily been spending time had been found wanting.

From then on, she was to find herself being more selective in her choice of society. She did not stop going to parties, for the very idea of a night gone by without at least some kind of amusement left her feeling bored and abandoned. But before she set off for anywhere, she now inquired as to who else would be there. The circle of people who were not to her taste grew ever larger, while those with whom she could actually enjoy herself became a rather exclusive small band. The other members of this band, as they all discovered to their mutual and common delight, felt exactly as she did. The words "drag" and "hassle" became a commonplace of their conversation, a special shorthand referring to the tacit understanding of the whole group that mood was a delicate creation, subject to constant interruption and blighting from those who were in

119

any way not finely attuned to it. What they called parties tended more and more to become gatherings no larger than could be comfortably accommodated in the bedroom of the host or hostess. The friendships among them were becoming ever more intimate, the relations between the girls and the boys ever more open and fluid—the term they themselves used was "human"—and time spent exclusively with one another ever more frequent.

It was here in the atmosphere of true and, as her parents had designated it in the course of one of their conversations, at last mature, friendship, that she achieved a full and proper introduction to marijuana. She had of course long since heard about the wonderful effect on mind and nerves of *Cannabis sativa*, and she had never entertained the slightest doubt that what she had heard was true. She had always known that such expedients as cough syrup or the downing of tablespoonfuls of ground nutmeg (a feat that she had never even attempted, finding so much as the smell of nutmeg repulsive to her) were merely juvenile substitutes for the headier experiences of real drugs. But drugs had intimidated her. She herself actually knew no one who used them. She had received a certain number of second- and third-hand accounts of nights of wild adventure with LSD, a hallucinogen said to be so powerful and extraordinary in its effect that one application could alter one's relation to the world forever. Her former friends in the rock band had proudly claimed intimate acquaintance with an older musician who, they told her in tones of awe, was a confirmed and incorrigible heroin addict. That was the point: drugs seemed so large, so final a commitment. It was said, in the passionate debate on the subject that had become one of the staples of press and television, that a week or even three days of taking heroin was all that was needed to make one a junkie, a figure of fear and revulsion, hiding from the law, from friends, from family, and suffering horribly. Pot, to be sure, was different. It was harmless, nonaddictive. Even the public officials who were moved violently to denounce it were capable of conceding, for example, that it was less harmful to the lungs and throat and blood circulation than tobacco.

Still, for one reason or another, the reasons being of no particular importance, she had up to this point remained a marijuana virgin. Largely, she supposed, it was that the stuff had not been very readily available. It was illegal; a certain amount of trouble had to be gone through to locate the supply and make the purchase; and, she was constrained to remind herself, she had after all been wasting a great deal of time and energy on the effort to have a good time with people who could now be seen to have been too callow and inane to distinguish silly child's play from the real thing.

In any case one night during a gathering in her room—she was tickled by the thought that she was in the end doing as her parents admonished and setting off on an escapade in her own home—she and several of her friends "turned on" for the first time. They had been supplied with a couple of cigarettes containing the magic weed by a recent newcomer to their circle, a young man who was a freshman at a nearby college and had become the lover of one of the girls. He instructed them thoroughly in the arts of marijuana use; and as the clumsy little hand-rolled cigarette, heavy with saliva, was passed around from mouth to mouth, as the deep inhalings were taken, held within the throat and chest, and sparingly released, as eyes rolled upward and heads sank back against the nearest support, she began at last to glimpse the state toward which all her earlier efforts had only been aspiring.

She experienced an odd tingling of the lips and

tongue—she could not say that it was altogether pleasant, but her cicerone told her that it was only the last gasp of her resistance and would soon go away—and a sensation in her arms and legs that made them feel at once both very heavy and very light and that was extremely pleasant. The sound in the room become slightly muffled and hollow, almost as if she had been transported somewhere outside it. She felt far away, untouched and unmoving and very, very happy. Later, everyone would speak of the way time had seemed to stop, so that a minute had taken on the weight of an eternity; the way they had heard things in the music—the fixed and standard accompaniment of all their leisure hours—that they had never heard before; the way they had seen the colors in the room, the starlight, one another's faces, as they had never seen them before. She would feel impelled by politeness to say such things as well, for agreement, consensus, shared experience were the very lifeblood of their fellowship, but she had not in fact had anything of this kind happen to her. Deep inside her, almost but not quite hidden even from her own view, she suspected that her friends' descriptions of their altered state of consciousness had been taken from the newspapers. Be that as it may, however, she had been overwhelmed, if not by singular visions and flashing lights, then by a far more important sense of being in some new kind of place where all was soft and easy. She did not particularly want to move but felt, on the other hand, that with no strain or effort whatever her body would have been able to perform any conceivable thing she asked of it. She was no longer able even to imagine the sensations of rage or shame or self-reproach; whatever she was, or had done, or would do, seemed good to her. Her friends had somehow receded from her, though they were all still very much present, and through the odd new distance between them she felt a great surge of tenderness and comprehension. As the hours wore on, she found herself wishing that they would leave so that she might go off to sleep without having to come down from her new perch of tranquility.

She had been foolish indeed to entertain even the slightest nervousness about pot. How could anything have been simpler than her submission to this flood of well-being? How could anything be more wholly benign, more healthy, more life-giving than a substance which could so directly and immediately and so without any possibility of ill effect miniaturize all one's everyday cares? They agreed to meet on the following weekend and try their new pleasures on a picnic under the open skies.

For several weekends thereafter they met regularly for the conscious purpose of turning on, the company having been enlarged somewhat to include two or three other members of the college freshman's class and one or two students at her school whom she had barely known or noticed before but who had turned out to be faithful pot-smokers and ever-ready suppliers. She had been astonished to discover that these schoolmates of hers, whom she had once almost completely overlooked, were among the most interesting and congenial people she had ever encountered.

Then, as it was bound to do, the consciousness of their purpose began to fade. They became accustomed users and needed no further planning or discussion or enterprise to set themselves in motion. Now when they gathered, joints were circulated among them without comment and their pleasures taken without examination.

Once they had a bit of a scare, when they were sitting together in a coffeehouse with a freshly lit joint passing from hand to hand and they saw, or believed they saw, a plainclothes detective eyeing them from a nearby table.

She was determined not to appear so childish as to say so, but for herself she was in fact rather thrilled to be taking part in such a wise and worldly exercise as recognizing a cop who was not in uniform. They managed to leave the place without incident. Another time they got into actual difficulty: one of the cars in which they were traveling collided with a parked car, causing a visible amount of damage to both. The driver had misjudged the margin of distance on his right. They debated what to do, since were they to wait and go through the proper procedure of reporting the accident, the aroma inside their car would have been telltale, and came to the conclusion that they had simply better drive off and work up some sort of explanation that would satisfy the driver's father.

But outside of these two incidents, there was very little left to mark off the smoking of marijuana as anything other than a perfectly organic part of their being together. Now and again a neophyte would be introduced to the group—one of the boys or one of the girls would bring along a date who was a stranger to them or to pot or to both—and there would once more be a small flurry of discussion about what they were doing and with what intended effect. More frequently, one of their number would be moved to discourse at length about some particular sensation or some powerful emotion that had been roused in him or her by that night's inhalations. Nevertheless, all real self-consciousness had vanished.

The young woman—for such indeed she now very much thought of herself as being—looked forward to these weekends with growing impatience. On the surface, her daily life was just as full as it had ever been. She still busied herself with companions at school, practiced for the driver's license that was one of the dearer wishes of her heart, browsed through the stores, worked her magic arts

124

before the mirror, held endless colloquia over the telephone, and in general kept herself engaged. Through it all, however, some part of her had come to feel stale and jaded. It was not just that a considerably smaller number of people now appeared to her to be acceptable or even merely tolerable playmates. It was not just that she was beginning to find a number of activities that had formerly seemed vastly amusing now somehow beneath her dignity. It was that life itself had taken on a peculiar new edge of boredom. Teachers imposed tasks on her that seemed not so much unjust as merely quite senseless. People—parents, relatives, neighbors, friends—had begun all at once, as it appeared, to ask things of her that were particularly irksome to fulfill. Everything had become an effort, bothersome and without sufficient return.

There were days when she simply did not feel well, with no particular symptoms she could name except a certain lingering distaste at the need to drag herself around. There were other days when she was jumpy, uncharacteristically quick to take offense, moving about quickly under the sway of some slight foreboding that each situation in which she found herself held the promise of trouble. But with the advent of the weekend, of the party that had come more and more to loom in her mind as a respite from the week's tiresome tribulations, she felt her spirits lifting. She could not wait to escape the uneasy regimen of living at the behest of others and, as she now thought of it, return to herself.

During the following year she was to wonder about what it was that had kept her at first so foolishly obedient to this weekly rhythm of boredom and release. It seemed to be nothing more than that a kind of routine had been established and that she had quite passively adopted it. In any case, there one day came the moment—she had just gone through some dreary contention with a boyfriend and had been unable to reach the girl in whom she was in the habit of confiding such matters—when it was borne in upon her that she need not deny herself the one solid comfort on which she knew she could absolutely rely. She sought out one of the students known to be a merchant in marijuana along with certain other medicaments and made her first private, independent purchase. From then on, she was no longer to be dependent on the backing and resources of the group for her forays into instant good feeling. It was almost as pleasant, she discovered, though far more direct and powerful and even somewhat disorienting in its effect, to turn on alone. She was, for instance, taking messages only from her own heart without the influence of others around her, and found herself doing things she had never done before. She went home and wrote a letter to her boy-friend, which she began as a letter of remonstration but which grew, through pages and pages of a rather irregular scrawl, to be a lengthy and profound essay on herself. Next she made her way to the rehearsal of the rock group which had once so abruptly rejected her—the group prac-ticed in the basement of a house across the street from hers—and requested to be allowed to sing. Finally, she took herself to one of the school hangouts and made some gesture of reconciliation to everyone present with whom she was in one way or another on bad terms. She was, she knew, not altogether in control of herself; and she felt marvelous.

Within days, she was turning on virtually every evening. Most of the time she had company, occasionally she was alone. When she was possessed of a fresh stock, she freely supplied the others. Sharing was a major principle in the special ethic of pot. When she had run out, there was al-ways someone equally ready to supply her. Marijuana was not expensive, certainly not when she considered the value received, but it did absorb some considerable part of her week's allowance. From time to time she found herself unable, without applying to her parents for extra money beyond the fairly generous allotment they were already providing, to indulge in her customary expeditions through the department stores. Shopping was anyway losing a good deal of its allure: instead of diverting, it tired her. She supposed she was getting too old to take much pleasure in merely contemplating all that vast variety of goods. She found that her feet began to drag through the aisles and her attention to wander quickly from the objects before her. Increasingly, she found that when she did go into a store she would simply buy things in a great rush, without considering. Nor could she easily bring herself to return anything she had purchased.

Her days in general became rather dreamy, although not always in a good sense. They seemed to go by, one after the other, with no clear definition of how they had been spent. Any problem that happened to arise could agitate her mind for hours. Headaches and eye aches, to which she had lately become subject, menstrual cramps, irritation, hurt feelings, disgust—all these could grow to a point where they felt as if they were completely occupying her being. On the other hand, the little moments of excitement and amusement, or of pride and pleasure in something she was doing, had a way of slipping right out of mind. Each morning she woke up feeling ever more reluctant to go to school. What had once seemed to her the day's adventure now seemed to her a block of time to be got through with a minimum of trouble or exertion, a time of floating, which need not necessarily be unpleasant but which touched her very little and partook very little in the quality of her real life.

Her mother and father had taken notice of the frequency with which she had lately begun to complain of physical distress. They had insisted that she see an eye doctor, who had found nothing essentially wrong and had given her a prescription for drops to ease what was evidently the strain of too much sun and study and television. She was given a course of treatments for sinus on the theory that a slight infection of the sinuses may have been the cause of her headaches; and when this had no effect, it was suggested that she may have developed an allergy of some kind, and she was given a series of antihistamine injections. Her mother took her to a gynecologist to ascertain whether her menstrual difficulty might be connected with some kind of female disorder. He could find nothing wrong with her, he said; perhaps her uterus was slightly tipped, but he would not for the time being recommend that anything be done about that; probably the whole thing would vanish—this he offered with an urbane grin—if and when she began to use the Pill. What concerned her parents most of all they could find no way of bringing to the attention of a doctor because it was so vague, and that was her languor. She spoke a good deal about being fatigued, and she looked fatigued. They began to pay attention to her diet, and they urged her to eat properly. They suspected, though it had not shown up on any tests, that she might be a bit anemic, and forced her to take iron and vitamin pills. She was obviously running too hard, they told her; come summer vacation, she had better think about taking it slow and easy.

She offered no resistance either to the doctors or to her parents on any of the questions concerning her health. She was at a loss to understand, however, why they moved with such alacrity to deal with all the minor matters of her life and at the same time were so persistent, so adamant, in what she could only take to be their refusal to understand the major things that were happening to her. They seemed on the one side blind to any perception of her difficulties that did not originate in their own view of things—saying to her with an assurance that was meant to be comforting but was in fact infuriating that her boredom and disappointments with her friends and disaffection with school would all quickly pass away when . . . when she went off to college, or variously, when she was something called "older" or "sure of herself" or "on her own." And on the other side, they dismissed, rather nervously, she thought, her hints to them about the new and genuinely releasing pleasure that had come into her life.

One evening she began to speak to them, more or less academically, about marijuana—about how many of her friends used it and the things they said about it—and all she received by way of reply was a discussion of the perils of engaging in activity that could bring the police down around one's neck. They pretended that they wished to know all about her, she thought bitterly, but in truth they only wished to know that which suited their own narrow and particular sense of life.

Nor, she discovered, was this the case only in her family. One of the subjects that received the most searching examination in the late-night conversations that had become a staple of her life in society was the subject of parents. The easy, open talk among her companions in pot had produced much fascinating material about the conduct and attitudes of mothers and fathers. There was very little, it seemed, that was unique or private in the resentment she was feeling toward her own. On the contrary, parents were a class. And whatever were their individual differences— some, for instance, fussed about the late hours their children were keeping, some did not; some evinced great hurt

at what they claimed to be a lack of communication between their children and themselves, some obviously preferred it that way; some railed against marijuana as they
did against all drugs, some, like her parents, pretended
not to notice—in the end they were all quite clearly pursuing a single class interest. The nature of that class interest
was, as she was getting older and more detached from
them, becoming ever clearer. They were defending their
own largely dull and miserable lives against the onslaught
of the new spiritual liberation of their children.

The main thing she and her friends were learning from
their ventures into naked consciousness was how little of
value or importance there was to be found in the life for
which they were being so carefully nurtured. All the struggle, self-denial, submission to regular daily routine, all the
troubles and worries, and even the petty, empty dumb-
show that passed for satisfaction, which were the sum and
substance of their parents' existence, now stood exposed
before their children as the Great Cheat of the so-called
ordinary respectable life. That was why so much of that ordinary respectable life as was being imposed upon her
these days had become intolerable. The true comfort of
marijuana was the comfort of knowing that the round of
endless striving which took place in the world out there,
the world toward which parents and families and teachers
were leading them, was not a higher order of reality but a
lower. The world which she and her companions had succeeded in opening up for themselves was a world in which
creativity and accomplishment and fellowship flowed naturally, almost as extensions of one's body, and therefore
operated by an entirely different set of standards for judging what was good and what was not and what was important and what was not. To have acknowledged the existence of this world would have threatened their parents

130

with the extinction of everything they stood for and had sacrificed their whole lives to obtain. Being "straight" was a form of cowardice, of running for cover, in the face of one's true instincts and animal nature. It was to be doubted whether parents had ever been capable of spontaneous acts of fun. It was to be doubted whether they had ever emptied out and contemplated the actual contents of their storage of thoughts and wishes. It was to be doubted above all whether they had ever for a single moment overcome their dead burden of social and sexual inhibition. Glimpsing such possibilities, now, in their children might throw not only their own private histories but their whole bustling civilization into chaos. More than one fit of helpless giggling had been set off among her circle by the attempt to imagine what this one's father or that one's mother would do if he or she ever turned on. Parents, however, were in truth no laughing matter. They spoke of love but were capable of loving only a single image of their own construction. It was not difficult to estimate how great must be the underlying hostility they harbored toward their offspring.

By her senior year in high school, then, she had grown so restless with the outer conditions of her existence that she found no peace except when she could shut them out. She was now turning on before she left for school in the morning, and then again before she set out for home in the late afternoon. The cigarettes puffed and passed around in the girls' bathroom were seldom any more of tobacco. She moved from class to class with great calm, withdrawn from the proceedings, almost always slightly aloof and dazed. She found, to her amused approval, that far from suffering, her schoolwork seemed to prosper. She sat quietly at the back of the classroom gazing out the window, and if she was called on to recite was always able to improvise something with an air of thoughtfulness that did a great deal to cover the fact that she had no very clear idea of what in particular was then under discussion. She had ceased to worry about tests, and discovered for the first time that she could write at length about virtually anything. As a result, she was doing rather better than she had ever done before. Her classmates, except for one or two of her closest friends, tended to shy away from her somewhat. Now and then this occasioned in her a certain ruefulness, but for the most part she was content to be left alone with her intimates.

At home, though, no such acceptable settlement was possible. She could not, it seemed to her, be left alone for a minute. No sooner had she situated herself comfortably—stretched across the couch contemplating the ceiling or behind the closed doors of her room preparing to savor an hour of sinking into her own thoughts or locked into the safety of the bathroom where she might commune with the sacred Weed—than one or both of her parents would invade her privacy with an anxious inquiry as to whether she was feeling all right. After a few displays of temper on her part, they ceased to ask the question in so many words but asked it nevertheless by the looks of anxiety they could or would not forbear from casting her way. No sooner had she curled up for a few hours of sleep, or rather that state of drowsing and daydreaming that was the entryway to sleep and which had become for her one of the sweeter ways of getting through empty time, than one or both of them would come by asking whether she needed anything. They had tried to explain to her their concern, but had come up with nothing better than that she appeared to them these days, for one of her age, to be singularly withdrawn and listless.

She knew better than they, of course, what was bothering them: her life had been set upon a course of ease and happiness that was alien to them and that offended their puritan sense of the value of grim achievement. They had long since found out about the marijuana, had extracted a promise from her not to overuse it, and had from that time forth been rather pitifully conspicuous in refraining from mention of the subject. Once they had gone so far— this outrage was one she had promised herself never to forget—as to suggest that perhaps she might wish to see a psychological counsellor of some sort. There could, she thought, have been no clearer or more final parting of the ways than that they should have classified the way she was living—at one with herself, in touch with her impulses, beyond the reach of pointless turmoil—as a possible form of illness. She longed to be able to avert her eyes from the spectacle of their envy.

The issue had come to a head with their discussions of the question of college. From one point of view, she had been excited by the thought of going away to school. The glimpse of freedom it afforded, of being able at last to chuck the society she had inherited and make one entirely of her own, of being able to live as she pleased without parental pressure and hostility, of being able to dress, eat, and fill her days in a state of accountability to no one, had roused her to a veritable fury of happy daydreaming. She had actually applied to a couple of schools, one in the Southwest, one in California. But the truth was, she finally realized, that going to college would inevitably involve her for four more years in at least some degree of submission to the standards and expectations of the straight world. What she had wanted was only to get away. When her acceptance arrived from the school in the Southwest, she turned the question this way and that, and after a night of deliberation, informed her parents that she had decided not to go to college after all. She was tired of school and needed a respite from it; had she not been certain that they would have made a terrible row, she might not even, given the way she felt, have remained to complete high school.

They asked her what she imagined she would do if she did not go to college, and the answer led to a complete disburdening of her thoughts about life. She was, she felt, being honest with them at last. Honesty between them had always been a point of great parental pride; let her parents, then, face its consequences as far as she was concerned. *Do?* she fairly shrieked at them, experiencing a sudden surge of new energy. *Do?* The very question proved their failure to understand the first thing about her, or her friends, or probably her entire generation, who had, despite the best efforts of all their parents and schools and even the government to trammel them, found out for themselves that the real problem in life was not what to do but how to *be*. What made them assume she would as a matter of course find it necessary to do anything? The trouble with them was that they did not even dare to imagine the possibility of living without concern for society's ideas of accomplishment. All they wished for her was that she should turn herself into a little replica of them. They couldn't bear the threat to their neat little lives in the thought that their child might be something other. They could not bear, in fact, to allow her to be just herself. She and her friends had their own ideas about what was a worthy accomplishment and what was not. Simply to love one another and themselves was worth everything the world out there had to offer and then some. What had adults ever shown them except how to get ulcers and make wars? She would tell them what she was going to do: just the opposite of what all of them had done. She was going to enjoy life and learn how to live with people. She left the room feeling cleansed and spent. She had a headache, and spent the rest of the day in bed.

They could not in all honesty say that they had been stunned or shocked by the things she had had to say to them. Despite her charge, made in youthful rage but after all conventional, that they did not understand her, they had not been altogether unmindful during the past two or three years of her growing attitudes. They were hurt, to be sure—more by the fact that she had wished to hurt them than by the specific things she said. But they were neither surprised nor, below the level where her injustice to them rankled, taken aback. They had prepared themselves for this moment. After all, they too had undergone periods in their respective lives when they had stormed against the force of their parents' expectations of them, when they had determined—and even announced their determination with an anger that had helped them to find courage— to lead their own lives as they believed they ought to do. The struggle of each generation to come out from under the one before it was an eternal and immutable struggle. Had it not always been their most sacred vow of parenthood that they would remember this and allow it to happen? What if not respect for the right to be a person in her own way had lain at the bottom of all their relations with the girl?

The time had come to admit to themselves that yes, they probably had sought to impose certain of their own weaknesses and shortcomings on her. Without meaning to do so, they no doubt had unconsciously communicated to her many of their little tensions, problems, their, as their daughter would have put it, "hang-ups." In a more important sense, they had, as she said—though not for the reasons she said—felt a resistance they had clearly been unable to hide toward her involvement with marijuana and the whole way of life this involvement seemed to imply. Marijuana had been strange to them; they had not been able to shake off the old associations it had for them with drugs and evil and the disreputable. So they had not deceived her in their attempts to treat the matter lightly. They were not, naturally, narrow-minded or defensive as she had accused them of being. They had followed very carefully all the expert discussion of marijuana, all the claims and counterclaims, all the allegations both for and against it. They were not to be numbered among the prissy members of their generation who liked to fancy that marijuana, or even stronger drugs, could in some way be morally distinguished from alcohol. Their ressistance to what they called "the pot scene" had been based on nothing more than the fact that it was alien to them. They worried about how she might one day make a living if she didn't continue on in school. They worried that she might one day fall into and suffer at the hands of benighted authorities. They worried about the way she seemed to be growing ever more careless with certain of the necessities of her health and physical welfare. Most of all, however, they had been reacting to the way marijuana had caused an interruption in the intimacy of the household.

But the only way such intimacy could return—they were grateful that they had the sense to understand—was through an honest tolerance on their part for her differ-

136

ences from them. If her way was not their way, if her values were not their values, if her needs were not their needs, this might be more than anything else a sign that they had successfully completed what they had set out to do for her, that is, bring her up to be her own person. And after all, it was true that many of her values had appeared to them for some time now to be fostering a new and wonderful kind of moral superiority. She may, for instance, have become what was by their lights downright slovenly, but how really, for people of sensitivity, could such a shortcoming be measured against the incredible generosity and gentleness with which she and her good friends treated one another? Could they not as parents even claim some small bit of credit for the way in which she preferred to take as little notice as possible of all the forms of outward show and concentrate instead on what was inner?

All of which in the end boiled down to: she had her life to lead, including her own mistakes to make. And there was reason to suppose that in some important respects she knew better how to do so than they once had.

Some weeks later, she came to them with a proposition: three of her friends, two girls and a young man, had decided to take an apartment together, where they could live in harmony without causing any further anxiety to, or being caused any further anxiety by, their families; and she wished to join them. If her mother and father were to add to her regular allowance only as much money as they would otherwise have paid for tuition to the school she did not wish to attend, she would be able to contribute her share of the rent.

They thought it would be a maturing experience for her, and approved of her desire to assume the responsibility. A bank account was opened for her, with the sole proviso that should she find such living difficult or in any way undesirable she not be proud and return home immediately.

When the apartment had been found and duly rented, her father put her things into his car and transported them to her new home. She did not wish him to bother with taking them up for her. They waved good-bye at the curb.

FOUR

The Sexual

Revolutionist

They simply could not get over how quickly and easily she had come to sexual maturity. It was almost as if she had become the embodiment of some kind of return to the state of nature. For they could not help being reminded by the very look of her, by the way she carried herself, and even by the way she had begun to think and speak, that but for the social complexities and interventions of modern civilization, she would after all by now have been a wife and mother. As it was, she was still a child in high school—but not, most definitely not, the world could see, a child at all.

Her mother, looking back over her own adolescence, could not remember a single case—and that very much included herself—of a girl of fourteen or fifteen who had been so poised and so relaxed in the face of nature's mes-·sage that she had just been thrust into the realm of sexual possibility. Her daughter seemed not to be frightened by it, nor overwhelmed by it, nor rendered in the slightest way gauche, giggly, shy, dirty-minded, or cruel, all of these last having once constituted a standard line of defense for young girls suddenly taken with the force of their own sexuality. Even her very physical development appeared to have been much eased and hastened: before they had had time to look around, so to speak, she had been positively hurtled into nubility.

Her father discovered, not without a little surprise, that he preferred not to look too closely or think too clearly about all this. To his amusement, but also to his real discomfiture, he was turning out to be rather more of a comic-opera father of daughters than he had ever anticipated being. But since he knew that his uneasiness was comic, and since he had of course immediately understood its Freudian origin, his reservations about facing up wholly to his daughter's new condition were not really serious. Somewhere beneath the surface layer of his discomfort he was perfectly aware, and also in his own way deeply impressed and pleased, that the girl was turning out to be an altogether self-assured and attractive woman.

The gracefulness and wholesomeness of her accommodation to sex was particularly apparent in her relations with boys. Indeed, with boys it could be simply said that she was on the best and friendliest of terms. She did not, naturally, like them all: that in itself was a mark of her wholesomeness, for she was not in the least what they used to call "boy crazy." Nevertheless, after only a brief interval, somewhere around the age of eleven, of viewing each and every one of her male contemporaries as "awful" and "mean and stupid," she had with no difficulty resumed a cheerful and pleasant comradeship with those of them she did like. They visited her at her home, she visited them at theirs. They hung around together after school, in couples or in groups, sometimes with flirtatious intent, sometimes

142

merely as friends. They talked freely together, in some degree were able to exchange confidences, performed small acts of mutual sympathy and consideration, and on the whole were as likely as not to behave as if they cared about one another in an ordinary human way. In other words, she was able to accept their company, and they hers, with very little of that nagging and unattractively anguished self-consciousness that had so bedeviled the contact between adolescent boys and girls in her parents' generation. Since she did not appear to fear these boys, or to hold them mysterious, the bearers of some terrible and as yet unnameable power over her, it was possible for her in turn to keep them from fearing, and so being ugly or aggressive toward, her.

Nor was her wholesomeness any less apparent in her relations with the girls who constituted her special circle of friends. With her girlfriends she had succeeded in establishing a mode of intimacy, of affection and loyalty, that quite dumbfounded her mother. The mother could to this day, for instance, in thinking of her own girlhood friendships, reexperience all the ill-concealed tensions of rivalry, all the petty meannesses and mutual betrayals: so customary a part of the social life of young women who, under the onslaught of burgeoning sexuality, had nothing left over for others in the struggle to capture some small sense of self. She was in a perpetual state of wonder, then, at the spectacle of the group life engaged in by her daughter and her female friends. So far from being rivals, the members of this group, with her daughter very much at its center, were staunch and loyal supporters of one another. So far from being mean or treacherous and competitive, they seemed genuinely to love and admire and depend on one another. The mother could only suppose that in some way this phenomenal ease about herself, about her body and its new capacities and desires, had opened up in her child a truly precocious gift for friendship. Being fundamentally at peace with herself as a newly full-blown female, the girl had been able to reach an unbelievably mature level of concern and generosity toward others.

Now, that their daughter should be found to be behaving with a maturity well beyond her years was no longer in the least astonishing to them. She had always, in both word and deed, displayed a sensitivity and an emotional wisdom way beyond the normal capacity of her age. Even as a very little child, consigned by all the most reputable psychological theory to being exclusively preoccupied with herself, she had displayed an understanding and responsiveness to the feelings of those around her that had time after time fairly taken their breath away. Still, the particular kind of maturity that was betokened by her ease in dealing with the attitudes and manners surrounding sexuality was in their opinion an entirely different matter. This involved a good deal more than merely intelligence or responsiveness. In one so young as she, they felt, it was no less remarkable than would be the sight of a tiny, light canoe gliding smoothly through a raging rapids. Here she was, having passed through what had always been a trauma of greater or lesser proportions—a shock, an upheaval, even for those who, like themselves, had one day managed to come out of it (if they might say so themselves) in pretty handsome shape. For her the whole thing had quite clearly been no more than the next welcome item on life's agenda.

They often discussed the question of why this should have been so—in deference to the father, of course, only in the most general of terms. How was it that their daughter, and they along with her, should have been blessed with so serene a passage into womanhood? It was not that they were in the least inclined to look a gift horse in the mouth. But the matter, they knew, was likely to have a very central bearing on the issue of her future happiness. Naturally, it was a difficult question to answer in any single, sim-ple way. Perhaps, they told one another jokingly, the serenity they were enjoying now was a kind of restitution from the gods for the nearly intolerable turbulence of her infancy. Perhaps the anxiety and travail they had suffered in her first year of life, when she had cried day and night for months on end and they had paced the floor with her, nearly beside themselves with fatigue and care, had been merely an investment on which they had had to wait twelve or thirteen years to be repaid. More seriously, it no doubt had a great deal to do with the girl's own character and personality: with her delightful openness and venturesomeness of spirit, not to mention her great lusty appetite for all things grown-up and sophisticated. At each point in her life she could not seem to wait, had champed at the bit, for the arrival of something new.

Explanations of this kind, however, somehow by themselves did not suffice. No one could be more cognizant than they of all the ways in which their daughter was in her own right a most superior young girl. Moreover, they had always carefully avoided trying to claim credit for her virtues—as their own parents had always either openly or tacitly claimed credit for everything that pleased them about their children, thereby leaving nothing to the children's account but their shortcomings. Still, it was in this instance impossible for them not to believe that some important part of her success had inevitably to be attributed to them.

They would never say such a thing arrogantly or boastfully, but rather entirely in a spirit of relief, grateful for everything they had at last been able to accomplish. Because whatever its pleasures and satisfactions, for them parenthood had not been what they could call an easy proposition. The whole process of bringing up a child had from the very beginning revealed itself to them as a thoroughly delicate, complex, and dangerous undertaking. Mindful of having been granted a possibility never granted to parents before—that is, to be able to see straight into the workings of the human mind and heart—they had not for one moment in dealing with their child been able to set aside the burden of knowing that everything they did was bound to have some form of lasting consequence for her.

If they were on the one side members of the first generation to be liberated from a whole host of silly concerns and superstitions, the kind of silly concerns and superstitions that had subjected parents to a needless and punishing fear, they were on the other side members of the first generation to understand how real and weighty was their true power over the psychic development of their children. Being conscious of that power was, to be sure, providing them with a wonderful opportunity. How much nonsense, how much pointless and futile impediment to happiness, could they not now eliminate from the collection of psychic baggage that future generations would be asked to carry? But by the same token, the consciousness of power had given them a sense of responsibility that their own mothers and fathers had all too evidently been spared. And this sense of responsibility had borne down upon them endlessly with the need to consider whether at any given moment they were thinking, saying, or doing the correct thing.

Nowhere, of course, had such power and responsibility been greater than in the area of sex. In fact, they were prepared to believe that parental influence on the child's feelings about sex was in the end the only kind of parental influence that really mattered. After all, it was fair to say— indeed, it had been one of the highest triumphs of their

age that people could now say—that an individual's relation to himself as a sexual being defined and determined
his relation to everything else of any importance. Thus the
satisfaction they took in seeing their daughter free of all
that had so beclouded, besmirched, taken the joy and
healthy high spirits out of their own introduction to sex
was a far from breezy one. And they did not fail to find it
all the greater for that.

But whether they were inclined to feel boastful about
the fact or not, it was certainly true that the foundation for
their daughter's present fortunate state had been laid
down for her years and years before—before she herself
had ever given the subject of sex or anything remotely related to it a thought. It had been laid down first of all, and
no doubt most importantly of all, in the ideas that they had
had about what would be necessary to her welfare. They
understood, as others before them had never had the
courage to understand, that sex in human affairs was no
incidental or isolable phenomenon but rather the driving
force behind most if not all emotion and activity. A healthy
mind and even a healthy body depended on one's capacity
to live in harmony with it, and this capacity in turn depended on the acceptance of its dominion over oneself
without fear or shame, above all without shame. Mankind's resistance to the force of sex, born in ignorance and
taboo and the impulse of organized religion to deny its ad-
herents their innocent pleasures, had led to a notion of the
body as somehow loathsome and unclean; and this notion
had served for century after century to twist the sexual
appetites of men and bury or extinguish altogether the
sexual desires of women. Few had escaped unscathed or
untormented. They themselves, while they had grown up
in a world on which the grip of sexual taboo had by comparison with the past already been considerably weak-

147

ened—thanks to the heroic labors of a lonely band of doctors and philosophers—had had to work with all the powers of reason and self-discipline they could muster to overcome the shame that had been their birthright. The father, though before his marriage he had suffered little shy-
ness in his pursuit of women, was to this day somewhat put
off by the vision of their unseen complicated machinery of
reproduction. And during that first unaccustomed and
uncertain year of marriage, the mother had found it useful to seek out some professional help in establishing and
putting forth her demands for erotic gratification. They
could say now with great pride and satisfaction that sex
had been given its proper due in their lives, but the process had required of them, and to some extent continued to
require of them, a good deal of earnest and disciplined endeavor. Their child—they had decided the point long before she had ever been conceived—would be put at no
such disadvantage. She would be taught to accept her body
as she accepted the daylight, and she would be allowed to
savor all its pleasures, from the very cradle on, without any
interference from whatever remained of their own sickly
fastidiousness.

But it was not enough to expound the doctrine of liberating sexuality: one had to make very sure that no vestigi-
al problems of attitude—betrayed by a chance remark, a
look on the face, a tone of voice—had survived to give the
lie to that doctrine. Children, it had been another of the
glories of the age to recognize, were more sensitive to atmosphere than to detail. Where their own interests and
feelings were concerned, they could discern what was truly
being communicated to them beneath any amount of verbal elaboration. Thus it would not be enough to tell their
child that she was to be freed of sexual inhibition, to issue,

as it were, her emancipation proclamation; they would have in attitude and deed actually to free her.

And free her they had. If the foundation had been laid in their ideas, it had been cemented in their behavior. Nothing relating to sex, neither infantile masturbation nor childhood curiosity about the body nor the little girl's need for information about life and love and reproduction, had either been shut off or obscured in a fog of their embarrassment. When she was little, even her father had actively participated in the process. Later, when he began to be beset by feelings of reluctance he could not control, he stepped into the shadows and let her mother carry on.

Her explorations of and comments upon her own body were greeted with a cheery though respectful welcome. When these explorations were extended to others, particularly to her little playmates, they thought it the better part of policy to stop her lest she bring down upon her head and be severely traumatized by the stern reaction of parents less enlightened than they. Their intervention, however, did not take the form of indicating to her that she had done something "wrong"—she might then all her life, as they had, connect her innocent sexual curiosity with shame. They simply changed the subject, distracted her by introducing a new and especially appealing activity. Their own bodies were also fully available to her inquiry. Genitalia, both male and female, were given their proper educated names and specified as to function. They found it interesting to note that with her parents she never overstepped the bounds of visual and verbal inquiry and never seemed to wish to. It was as if nature had provided her with an instinct for drawing lines of limit around that which nature itself had solemnly interdicted.

No point was ever made with her about nudity, and

again, till nature itself had seemed to draw a line within her own spirit, she ran about the house, on the beach, even in the playground, with no apparent consciousness of whether she was clothed or not. They were enchanted by her lack of self-consciousness. Sometimes it seemed to them that they had spawned a sprite rather than a child, and they feared to speak one word about the matter of her covering herself, lest they be responsible for slamming down the shades of the prison-house.

So open and unaffected was her relation to all this, indeed, that they could not have said at what point or at what age she had been taught the facts of life. Her formal sex education had begun on the very first occasion when she had asked them where babies came from—probably she was three or four years old—and had proceeded on continually, with an ever larger, ever more complex supply of facts as she grew old enough to comprehend them, until there appeared to be nothing further she had left to learn.

Along with shame, shame's handmaiden, ignorance, had formerly been the most powerful agent of sexual repression; their daughter's emancipation depended not only on the free development of her natural feelings but also on the condition that her mind not be buried beneath a litter of half-baked notions and misinformation. This, too, had become evident to all the doctors and experts of the soul who were busily uncovering the major sources of human misery. For one thing, the very fact that here was a subject about which she was being left with great lapses of knowledge would communicate to the child that sex must inherently be something forbidden. For another thing, the sex act itself was diminished and those who engaged in it left short of the highest possible fulfillment, by the simple lack of knowing all the chemical, biological, and physiological forces that were coming into play. The mother and father both knew the truth-of this last observation on their very pulses. It was not for nothing, they reflected, that the book which had once been the Bible for newlywed couples determined to burst the shackles of a constricting sexual upbringing, written by a kindly Dutch gynecologist named Van der Velde, devoted the whole of its opening section to a straight recapitulation, with charts and diagrams, of the reproductive process and its organs.

Naturally, their little child would not for years either wish or be able to master all the physiological subtleties of sex, but it was imperative that everything she did wish and would be able to master be precisely the same truth only more simply told. That was why after their first tentative conversations with her in which they imparted the news that babies for some time before they were born lived in their mommies' tummies, they purchased a book to be read to her whenever any further questions arose. Such a book would be a far better means of instructing her than their own extemporaneous efforts, they decided, because it would tell her, as they might mistakenly fail to do, neither less than she needed to know nor more than she was prepared to understand. They were terribly impressed with the book which, after consulting the bulletin of the Child Study Association or some such publication, they had bought. "Did you ever," began the chapter on sexual intercourse, "notice the dogs who run about and play in your backyard?" (Their daughter had always been particularly fascinated by dogs, and they thought this the most fortunate of coincidences.) "Sometimes the male, or daddy, dog climbs with his forelegs onto the back of the female, or mommy, dog. They are making a baby." The text was accompanied by an appropriate drawing. The first time her mother had read to her from the book she had been fascinated, sitting absolutely still and silent as she rarely sat during one of their reading sessions, poring without comment over the illustrations, nodding her head each time her mother asked her if she understood so far. They noticed, however, that she never by herself asked to be read to from that particular book again. Now and then her mother would suggest it, and she would, more dutifully than anything else, it seemed to them, agree.

At some point it occured to them that the ways of nature were far more vividly revealed through the actions of nature itself than through words or concepts. And since she had shown a certain enthusiasm for contacts with animals, they bought her a male and a female rabbit. She would look after the animals, was the idea, or at least help in the looking after them, and thus in the most ordinary, matter-of-fact way become privy to the whole cycle of reproduction. She loved the rabbits dearly, but as pets they were a disaster. They dirtied the house, refused to be tamed, and whether because of some disease or whether the parents had been cheated into buying two rabbits of the same sex, the animals insistently refrained from providing the child with an opportunity to witness birth. The rabbits were followed by guinea pigs, who did reproduce but struck terror to the little girl's heart because the day after the first litter was born, the male, whom they had not known they had to isolate from his offspring, brutally attacked and killed one of the babies. That, too, said the father, in an effort to reassure his wife that they had not permanently scarred the little girl, was a part of nature. It was not, to be sure, the aspect of nature they had hoped to introduce her to, but it after all could not be left out, either. In any case, in the end she recovered splendidly, and though some of her appetite for pet-keeping had waned, she did very nicely incorporate within her general sense of life that firsthand observation of parturition and motherhood.

Finally, there was that part of her education—in some sense, of course, the most important part—which had proceeded informally from the very circumstances of her daily life. This had to do far less with what her parents, and later teachers, and in fact the whole world that surrounded her told her than with what parents and teachers and the surrounding world refrained from telling her. She was sometimes told that expressions of open sexual curiosity were "inconvenient," as, for instance, in the presence of her grandparents, but she was not ever told that they were naughty. She was also not told, either outright or by those sudden eloquent interruptions of adult conversation when she entered a room, that she was too young to understand anything she desired to understand. She was never publicly shamed for any species, direct or indirect, of sexually oriented behavior.

And what was perhaps for a little girl the final and crucial promise of tolerance for her future erotic drives, she was never cordoned off in an entirely special province called femininity. Though there were certain conventions of dress and play which associated her squarely with her mommy rather than her daddy, nothing in her childhood upbringing imposed upon her the need to be something once referred to as "ladylike." The demands of ladylikeness had been a kind of basic training in the postures of chastity; its rules and manners and attitudes had constituted the social analogue to a calm and cool frigidity in bed. To treat one's child to the disciplines of being a lady was to set her aside from the noisy, sweaty, thrusting world of masculine enterprise, and with it, of naked lust and eroticism. No such discipline had ever even been hinted to her. Certainly, she had never been instructed to sit, stand, walk like a lady—the very thought of it made her parents giggle. Nor had the issue of good manners or good taste ever been proposed to her with any connection to gender. If she were cautioned on the use of obscene language, for instance—which rarely happened anyway—she would be told not that such words were not nice for a little girl but that there were people in the world who for one reason or another were likely to take it into their heads to be offended by them and that it was not kind to give needless offense. If she were scolded for hitting her playmates or speaking nastily to them or scuffling with them over some disputed toy, again the censure would be offered solely on the grounds that such behavior was unkind. Even the conventions of female dress and recreation had undergone a serious weakening of force. She played with dolls, she played "house," she got herself up in her mother's old gowns and shoes and trimmings, but with no greater frequency, and indeed with considerably less frequency, than that with which she ran around among gangs of boys and girls together throwing things, hitting things, climbing things, and shouting at the top of her voice. Moreover, it was only at birthday parties and family occasions of some solemnity that she was ever seen in a dress. She did not object to wearing dresses, in fact rather liked it; but the community had decided, and her mother gratefully along with it, that there was no need to hamper her full choice of activity and in addition burden the household with a troublesome attention to frills by keeping her in a senseless, old-fashioned, and impractical everyday wardrobe. From her infancy on she had, indistinguishably from all the little boys, gone about her active life in a pair of blue jeans and a polo shirt.

Crudely speaking, her parents imagined, all this could be laid up to the notion of political equality for females, to the battle waged and won in a somewhat misty past in order that she might vote, be educated, and follow a career.

154

There was no longer, for example, the smallest margin for discussion about the propriety of coeducation or of steady intimate contact between boys and girls as playmates, classmates, or good friends. They could not even conceive of the terms in which such a discussion might be seriously carried on, though they were aware that it had once, and not too long ago in history, actually been thought to be a discussable problem.

For themselves, however, they tended to be of a rather profounder cast of mind. They did not minimize the significance of the political element in an alteration of a way of life, but they were far more interested in its deeper psychic sources. Therefore it was clear to them that what they were witnessing—and if the real truth be told, what they were very much helping to carry out—was something far beyond and anterior to the mere "emancipation" of women. What they were witnessing in their daughter was the completion of a process, begun with them, for the emancipation of sex itself. The pulsing, driving force of this most radiant of all human energies would simply not, despite all efforts to do so, be held in check. If repressed, it sickened; what better demonstration of this proposition was needed than the history of the nineteenth and twentieth centuries? Sex, like water, was always seeking its own level. This little girl of theirs, at work and play in a manner not so very distinguishable from that of the little boys, was in fact not so distinguishable from them. Though her future was bound to be in one crucial sense different from theirs—she would be a mother and a keeper of the hearthfires—in another crucial sense there would be no difference at all. She would lust as they would, require the satisfaction of a sexual demand as they would, and find either health or sickness depending on how great or small was the degree to which she provided herself that satisfaction. That girls and boys spent most of their waking hours together, then, that the same standard of conduct was applied to them, in school as well as at home, that they dressed alike, spoke alike, and were encouraged to think alike, was not just the result of a new social or political style. It was the truth about the inner life of the sexes at last revealed.

Nor had they for one moment permitted themselves to forget, though the father had vastly preferred not to talk about it, that their view of their daughter's sexuality had its simple, practical consequences. A child brought up to live in a healthy relation to her body was a child whose actual sex-life was bound to be an active and carefree one. They certainly wished for her one day to be married and settled down, for that of course was an essential of happiness, but as things had worked out in modern society there was an inevitable gap of many years between the onset of sexual desire and the arrival of the proper time for marriage. There were no grounds on which to demand that she deny herself the pleasures of sex until by some purely arbitrary legal and economic definition she were to become a full-grown woman. There were no grounds for such denial, and they had no wish that she be denied, in any case.

There was nevertheless, they found, a certain discomfort in the thought that she was being set adrift with no well-marked course in the sea of sex. They had begun to wonder which of the still-ungainly young men would provide her with her first crossing and to hope that he would not be too ungainly. Their conversations about her sometimes became what they themselves felt to be improper, skirting the edges of an imagery that had the power to disquiet them with its violation of her privacy. Even the mother, who had found the thought of her daughter as a sexual being perfectly easy to take, grew slightly uneasy when

156

that thought promised to appear in her mind in too specific a shape. They were inclined to forgive themselves for any feelings of discomfort, however, much as they believed they should not have them, for they understood how much of that centuries-long crippling tradition must still hold sway over their semiconscious life. The father, of course, was mainly stuck with an Oedipal impulse he could not be expected to overcome; and the mother was no doubt still being the victim of an early conditioning of her nervous system in which her mind and heart did not at all participate. And after all, what really mattered as far as their daughter herself was concerned were the things they said and did, not those that were the illegitimate residue of a history they could do nothing about.

What they said and did, they were very careful to make sure, provided not a breath of real hindrance to her freedom. Yet there was one anxiety about her that was, they felt, more than legitimate. Being put in the way of sexual activity, she was also put in the way of the possibility of pregnancy. They knew that she had a firm grasp on the purposes and modes of contraception, for they had taken good care to include such information in their sexual teachings. But young girls could not, alas, be counted on to be sufficiently concerned about the possible consequences of their impulsive behavior. So the parents worried, and delivered many more than one stern lecture, and told her horror stories about girls in trouble, and moralized in completely unequivocal fashion about the piteous ruination of lives—all from the failure to exercise an adult sense of responsibility.

Finally the mother came to the conclusion that lecturing her daughter on the subject of responsibility was in a certain sense an evasion of her own. Life had been organized in a distorted way: her daughter was coming to be a wom-

an, entitled to a woman's most important expression of being, and at the same time by remaining circumstance still a
very young girl, entitled also to a young girl's lighthearted-
ness about the future. The way to make sure that she did
not get herself pregnant was not by preachment but by
helping her to avail herself of the means to prevent it. On
the girl's fifteenth birthday—it was a private, loving joke
between them that this was really her birthday present—
her mother took her to the gynecologist. This doctor was
an ardent believer in the Pill. He assured them both that
rumors about the Pill's possible harmful effect had no truly
scientific base; though he would never say so in public, he
suspected that most opposition to the Pill was based in a
deep, unconscious hostility to sex and the belief that it
should at the least carry some genuine risk of punishment.
People hated the Pill because, whether they knew it or not,
they hated the idea that sex should at last have become
safely and freely available to the young.

Contraception, reflected the mother, had of course been
one of the important missing terms in the bourgeois ideology of no sex without marriage. Without a way to prevent
the world from being peopled with hordes of illegitimate
children, how could families allow their young daughters
even to entertain the possibility of sexual relations? Had
she herself not quaked at the prospect that her daughter
might become pregnant? The Pill was more than an effective means of contraception, as, having herself begun to
use it, she had recently discovered. The Pill meant that one
was free for sex without any preparation, without the consciousness of intention that using a diaphragm, say, always
involved one in, and without the interruption of one's ar-
dor by the necessary sober thought for tomorrow. With
the Pill, sex could just happen; she and her husband had

embarked on what seemed to them a whole new life together thanks to that simple realization.

As the doctor wrote out the daughter's prescription, her mother could not resist one small pang of envy. She did not know whether her daughter yet had need of this new medication or not, and did not want to know, since it was up to the girl to decide how much of her life in sex she wished to share with her parents. (They hoped, they were to tell her laughingly over her birthday celebration dinner, it would not be *too* much.) But now her daughter would never in her whole life know either the sickening need to hide and dissemble before her mother, such as she had once so painfully lived with, or that one last ineradicable bit of anxiety that women before her had always carried into bed. Her daughter, in other words, would never know how lucky she was. But that, too, she told herself in the very words her husband had used about the guinea pigs, is a part of nature.

The first time she had sex with a young man, it was she who took him to bed rather than the other way around. He was older than she, a university student, and lived by himself in a furnished room. She did not know if she liked him very much. Aside from those times when they were clenched in one another's arms, he was not particularly amiable or pleasant, and though he had a reputation for being terribly intelligent, he seemed to her to be somewhat dull company. She thought about him all the time, however, which was a rather new experience for her, and she certainly liked the idea that he was so much older than the boys whom she saw every day in school. She had contrived to have him meet her once or twice in front of her school building and had made a point of introducing him to a number of her classmates, and even to a teacher who happened to be passing by.

Aside from their rather gymnastic transports—they would move, without parting mouths, from wall to bed to floor to chair—they had also spoken about sex a great deal. She had informed him that she was a virgin, and he had repeatedly and patronizingly announced that virgin was a bad thing to be. She had discoursed on the subject of what she wanted from a sexual relationship, and with hooded eyes he had snickered at her for being an innocent square. Hence he had puzzled her a little. For the worldly attitude he adopted when he spoke to her did not seem to carry over into his conduct. She was eager to be divested of her virginity, eager, as she actually put it to herself, to "have it over with," eager to be translated into that attractive kingdom of the experienced which she had heard so much about, and she had imagined that this would be accomplished simply by surrendering herself. Yet, moaning and sighing and whistling through his teeth to indicate that he was approaching the boundary of the uncontrollable, he made no move to consummate their lengthy exercise in arousal. One evening she had put the matter to him delicately and he had stared up at the ceiling and told her that he was too old for child's games: any woman with whom he was to become involved in a real and serious sexual relationship would have to volunteer herself to him. He had no interest in seducing a young girl and then having to carry the burden of her endless whining and guilty feelings. She rushed out of his room mightily offended, but on later reflection came to be more and more engaged by the challenge he had thrown out to her. She was, she had by this time decided, in love with him; if she had little of what she would call fun in his company, that was because he was

160

so much more mature and manly than the young boys with whom she had formerly spent her time. His problems were real problems, and his thoughts about them were deep. She had always been considerably older than her age, and being with him had set off a whole new resonance of womanly intelligence and sympathy in her. The morning after she had taken such violent offense at the things he said to her, she telephoned him and said she had thought it all over and was volunteering. He was busy that day, he said, finishing up some work; she should come to his room the following afternoon.

Her defloration was completed rapidly, so rapidly she could not conceive of what the fuss had been about, either on her part or on his. Something told her this would not be an appropriate time to tell him that she loved him. Many times in the course of their relations some hunch or instinct of this kind would rise to restrain her, she would not quite know from where, and it would always prove to be trustworthy. She was not disappointed in the sex part of the occasion because she was well aware from everything she had read and heard that sexual pleasure was something it took time to cultivate, but try as she might, she could not help feeling a little disappointed that he on his side had so little to say to her. What would she have wanted? Perhaps only some small gesture of affection. Perhaps even just a postmortem to mark the significance of this afternoon in her life. But he had risen quickly from the bed, gone into the bathroom to wash, and slipped into his clothes. She had, she told herself, taken his dare, and she must surely not show herself unable to live up to it now. So she, too, simply got up and got dressed. And as soon as it was feasible to do so, they escaped the silence by rushing off to a soda fountain for a Coke. He did not say so, but she knew that now she was his girl.

All this had happened a very short time before her birthday visit to the gynecologist. Her mother's announcement that she was taking her there struck her as a truly fortunate coincidence. Because all those parental lectures about caution had had a powerful effect on her, and yet for some strange reason she had felt reluctant to inform her mother that the time had come when she had need of birth control. She did not mean to keep her affair a secret—such an idea had not even occurred to her—it was just that she had no desire to take her mother into her confidence in this way. She began to take the pills without making any mention of it.

Her girlfriends, of course, were a very different matter. They knew that she had been seeing the university student because nothing in any of their lives went unreported to the group. She told them what he had said to her about refusing to play the role of seducer, and though she felt it wasn't altogether nice to do so, noted with great pleasure the look of envy in the eyes of some of them during the account of her response. One of her friends, who had acquired something of a reputation as the neighborhood bad girl—and had had to sneak off all alone to the Margarent Sanger clinic, thinking she was required to tell them she was married and using an assumed name—sighed bitterly at her story of the session in the gynecologist's office. But mainly she was happy to have their support and the opportunity to discuss her feelings with people who could understand exactly how she felt—both of which she recognized that she very much needed.

After that, she and her lover were, except for the hours they had to spend in school, virtually inseparable. They went everywhere together, they ran errands and looked after their respective daily obligations together, they studied together in his room—she typed his papers and he tutored her in mathematics—and she spent the night with him at least once a week. This she did at first by deceiving her parents into thinking she was staying over with a girl-friend. She could not have said exactly why she found it necessary to deceive her parents. They were not ignorant of how much time she was spending with her lover and gave her every reason to believe that they understood pretty largely what was going on. Nevertheless, to her sur-prise, she still had certain reservations about them. Mostly she feared that they would ask her questions, and she was not yet prepared to discuss her situation with them in any detail. Her delicacy on this point was perforce to be brought to an end in the summertime, when he decided not to return home to his family and she had to sue for permission to move into his room full time. As things were to work out, however, his lodgings were to prove far too uncomfortable for two people to share in the heat of sum-mer. In any case, the cat would by then, as it were, be out of the bag. In the meantime, having moved so completely into his orbit, she saw very little of her own friends outside of school. Exchanges of confidence had to be accom-plished quickly in the hallways or at the lunch table, and now and then in leisurely sessions on the telephone. They understood, of course, and offered her no reproach. It was an unwritten agreement among them that one's sex life took precedence.

On that question, the question of their sex life, she and her young man had also settled into a state of unwritten and largely unspoken agreement. They made love dutiful-ly almost every day, and had ceased almost entirely to talk about it. More than anything else, she was gratified by the spectacle of his overheated need for her. In an otherwise somewhat uncertain and anxious atmosphere—for he had never grown to be really pleasant and affectionate—his sudden surrender to the pressure to make greedy use of her never ceased to make her feel strong and wise and in control.

When they talked, which they did, as it happened, a great deal, they talked not about sex but about the interaction of their characters and personalities. They discussed what it was that each was giving—or, if they were quarreling, what each was failing to give—the other. She was of a generally sanguine turn of mind, to be sure not nearly as sophisticated or conversant with the world as he, but on the other hand essentially more poised about confronting her problems. Sometimes, in a tender mood, he told her how much he valued and was benefited by her childlike innocence. Sometimes, and as the months wore on it got to be more and more often, he told her she was not bright or sensitive enough to understand him and that in her obedient little-girl credulity about the world she was like a millstone around his neck. She on her side was most admiring of his gifts; she called him brilliant and never ceased to wonder at how much he had enabled her to grow. Yet, she said, he was somehow emotionally blocked. He did not trust people and was afraid to give himself to them. She was so much younger than he, knew so much less, was so much less brainy, but still she had the capacity truly to love people and he did not. If he thought she was a millstone around his neck, might it not be useful for him to consider how very much in the way of emotional security he had taken from her and how very little returned? Usually, they concluded, even after the harshest of words had passed between them, that they were fundamentally very good for one another. They had, they would agree, as two individuals found an almost perfect dovetailing of needs and sufficiencies.

There were times when she hated him. These were the

164

times—they happened always in public—when he telegraphed to her the message that she was sexually inadequate. Sitting with friends in a bar or café, he would make an elaborate display for the assemblage of being smitten with the charms of some girl who happened to be passing by. He would turn his head to stare, roll his eyes, lick his lips, make noises of longing. Or at a party he would turn his back on her and throw himself into being uncharacteristically flirtatious and attentive to one of the other female guests, looking around only long enough to send her the most meaningful flicker of a glance—cold, pleased, and defiant. Once at a gathering she had stepped into the bedroom to find him sprawled out on the bed on top of her resisting and embarrassed and obviously unhappy best friend. She understood, albeit somewhat dimly at first, that all these displays were meant for her. She doubted that he did such things when she was absent. She was jealous, of course, but what moved her to hatred was his wish to humiliate her, to let her know in this way what he dared not speak in private: that she was not enough for him.

She was not sure, to tell the truth, what sexual adequacy meant. She knew all about the problem of frigidity, about women so afraid of sex or so repelled by it that they could not respond. She and her friends had a whole repertory of dirty jokes on the subject, and they had now and then, though only in a glancing way, even discussed it seriously with one another. From her own admittedly limited experience she could see how frigidity could turn the so delicately balanced, easily disrupted masculine enterprise of sex into a dreary chore. But she would not call herself frigid. Her pleasure in sexual intercourse was not uniform or reliable, and yet she thought of herself as a highly responsive woman. More than that, she had paid close attention to what it was that seemed to heighten her lover's pleasure and had usually sought to oblige him. She supposed she was no Tiger Lady—a thought that occasionally made her anxious—but then her lover was not exactly Terry and the Pirates either.

Here lay the true source of her hatred for him when he was in his mood of wanting to humiliate her. For deep down she knew, without being able to put her knowledge precisely into words, that if anyone were struggling with a problem of frigidity, it was he. His attempts to make her feel bad were almost like a child's declaration of independence. Something there was, of lust, of drive, of erotic savor, that was missing in him. She had taken him to bed the first time, and—there was no one to whom she could confess it, not even largely to herself—many, many, many of the times thereafter. His original refusal to have her unless she offered herself up to him had, with only an occasional exception, stood. If she had ever charged him with such a thing, he would have called her crazy. In the speed with which they usually glued themselves together, no naked eye could necessarily discern who had been the approacher and who the approached. Nevertheless, she knew what she knew. He was desperately hungry for sex most of the time, but he did not in truth like it all that much.

All this was to come to her only gradually, and even then with far from perfect clarity. And in any case, it comprised only the most inner, private part of their relations, a part that was generally forgotten in the glare of everyday business. Aside from their long discussions about themselves, which were almost always initiated by her and gave her the sense of a profound involvement with him, they spent a good deal of their time together in some kind of grown-up facsimile of play. They visited with friends, now and then threw parties in his room, read poetry together. In the summertime, each of them had a job. He watched over a computer, and she was a filing clerk, and they met each evening after work in the heaviness of the summer's heat for a hamburger and a movie.

All this was the part of her love affair that she liked the best. She liked belonging to him, being half of a couple whose existence was taken for granted by the entire world of their acquaintance. She liked being preoccupied with him, even when that preoccupation was a troubled or a hurtful one. She liked doing things for him—typing papers, running little errands, nursing him when he didn't feel well, soothing him when a professor or one of his superiors in the computer office or a particularly obtuse and insensitive friend had done or said something to ruffle his feelings. Though she often charged him with failing to trust people, she felt more and more that he was coming to trust her; and in some ways she liked best of all the way he called on her to minister to his various unhappinesses. From the other side, she, too, had been able to impose a number of her demands. The essence of love, she believed, was reciprocity, striking the balance between giving and taking. He gave her little of the kind of sympathy and reassurance she held in such ready supply for him, but she wanted and needed little—except sometimes. What she wanted was commitment, the knowledge that through thick and thin he would be hers, that she meant something to him and was not just an erotic convenience.

This, despite his occasional infuriating lapses into public display of lust for other girls, he gave her. All the time they were together she lived with the assurance that whatever plans he made, however large or small, she was included. He even gave her responsibility for managing his relations with his family, which were not of the best. They lived nearby, but he had long ago decided, and they had fully concurred, that it was out of the question for him to live at

167

home. A certain number of visits were mandatory, however, each of them before her arrival on the scene having routinely ended in some unpleasantness. Now he took her with him, in fact insisted on it; he would not go if for some reason she could not. She chatted away politely with his mother and father while he sat peacefully by. His father was quite smitten with her, and once or twice had not scrupled to give his son an insinuating nudge and wink; and his mother, though far more reserved about the situation, had declared the girl to be evidently a very good influence on her son. The son had laughed rather bitterly about this, but the girl had been secretly terribly pleased.

In the end, what pleased her most was the acknowledgment of her status in her own household. She had never actually come forth and announced to her parents that she was having a love affair. She had not, for instance, made further mention to her mother of the birth-control pills, nor had she taken her very much into her confidence about the way she was spending her afternoons and evenings. Still, the fact that her parents were not asking her about these things was an indication that they knew she now had a need for privacy and that they were prepared to respect it. She came and went completely as she liked. The young man frequently had dinner at her house and showed not the slightest hesitation about caressing her or speaking to her intimately in the presence of her parents. Nor had they shown even by so much as a flicker of the eyebrow that they were taking any notice. Her father would usually take himself off immediately after dinner to finish up some work or read or watch television, while her mother seemed quite content to stick around and make conversation with them, laughing and joking and being— the daughter thought she detected, but couldn't really believe it—rather seductive.

When the summer came, and they decided it would be good for them to live together outright, she simply told her parents what their plans were. She was delighted not only at the prospect of being able to be with him completely but at the immense feeling of freedom, of being a real person in control of her own real life, that this arrangement promised. She did not know whether her parents would object strenuously to it or whether the tactful respect they had been showing her would carry over into a recognition that she was entitled to do as she wanted. In her mind she marshaled all sorts of arguments with which to overcome their resistance, including, if it should be needed, the argument that they were nothing but a pair of hypocrites. But when the moment came to make them her announcement, her father merely sat enveloped in a sour quiet and her mother said yes. She was to call them every day and come home for dinner as often as possible.

She stayed with him, as it turned out, only for a couple of weeks. His room was airless, there was no space for her clothing, and on the really blistering nights his single narrow bed was a torture. Her room at home was large and air conditioned, and she returned to it. When her parents went away on a summer vacation, leaving her behind to her job and her lover, he moved into her house instead. After a time, it got to be a matter of mere preference where they slept.

On their return to school, they resumed their ordinary routine—only by this time he had become a kind of regular in the household and stayed overnight with her in her room pretty much as he pleased. Her parents expressed no opposition to the arrangement. On the contrary, they were, they told her, gratified that she found no need to sneak about, carrying on behind their backs as certain of her friends seemed to find it necessary or convenient to do behind the backs of their parents. To begin with, she accounted herself lucky. But oddly, her relations with her mother and father began to sour. She could not say what it was exactly, but she had begun to notice that their conversation seemed extraordinarily silly to her, and their responses to most matters that came up for discussion among the four of them, embarrassingly stupid. She contrived her best to have to spend as little time with them as possible. When they were together, she found herself speaking sharply and contemptuously to them. The look of hurt that came into her mother's eyes and the watchful supplication in her father's only added fuel to the flame. She was, she told herself, grown up now—a woman, with a woman's emotional responsibilities—and this seeing her parents in all their inadequacy was the inevitable result.

She was thinking about them a good deal. The more they went through the motions of understanding her experience these days, the less, infuriatingly, they seemed to understand. They seemed to believe, for instance, that she and her lover stood in danger of being driven beyond the bounds of all good sense by some maddening lust. They cautioned her to look after herself, protect herself, to make sure that she did not neglect her schoolwork or her health. They questioned her slyly about her emotional state, and, when they thought she wasn't looking, examined her with an unconcealed new curiosity. They were, in short, extremely dirty-minded. What deprivation, she wondered, what twisted, sickly perversion of mind and body had brought them to such a yearning, envious response to the presence of sex in the life of their child? She and her lover were not sex fiends but two healthy individuals enlarging and enriching what was a large and rich relationship. But pitying her parents for their evidently obsessive preoccupation with sex—as if it were one of the major

170

goods in life forever denied them—did not in any way mitigate her feeling of contempt for them. she would have preferred not to see the unfulfilled longing that made it impossible for them to imagine how she and her lover might spend countless hours together doing more important and valuable things than making love. Yet that was quite clearly what they did feel and did imagine. She heaved a sigh of relief that she would not have to go through life as they did, that sex could remain in its proper, healthy place. And as much as was possible, she avoided their company.

The affair was to last for something over two years, whether by coincidence or by unconscious design until she was ready to enter college. Technically, it came to an end in the course of a fight, one of many, but the last one. When she had stopped crying, and discovered that though bereft, she also felt hugely liberated from the burden of all his prickliness and passive cruelty to her, she recognized that this fight had not been a cause but only an occasion for their being extricated from one another. The plain fact of the matter was, she had grown and he had not. If anything, in allowing himself to be absorbed so naturally into the household by her parents, he had regressed. Though he was so much older than she, she had come to find him childish. She was looking forward keenly to going to college, and realized that in the back of her mind college had for some time been looming as the place where she would have the chance to meet young men far more interesting and exciting than he.

She consoled herself briefly for the loss of her lover with a boy encountered one evening at a party. She was conscious that not the least of his attractions for her was how unlike any of the young men she knew he was. He was young—her own age—handsome, rather slickly dressed, an excellent dancer, passionately devoted to sports, and he took her home on his motorcycle. Energy was only one of the things that distinguished him from her former lover. He spoke in an uneducated way, which had at first somewhat put her off and then pleased her, and he had only uneducated interests. No reading of poetry or contemplation of the cosmos was promised here. He lived on the other side of town, where, evidently, young men were still being kept in touch with the kind of vital passions that protected them from being sicklied o'er with the pale cast of thought. They might be a touch uncouth, but they made a girl feel like a girl. She judged his main passions to be wheels, females, and footballs, in, she told herself amusedly, roughly that order. The thought flashed through her mind—and was quickly filed away—that he had not likely met a girl like her before, either. She had caught a certain look of amazement and anticipation on his face when she began to utter, in the accents of purest refinement, her most earnest and colorful string of obscenities.

Since her parents were out for the evening, she gave herself to him on the living room couch. The whole thing was quite effortless and took no more than twenty minutes. She did not fail to notice both his astonishment and his gratitude at the coolly easy and wordless way she surrendered herself. The next day he called her and took her to the beach. They made love in the sand, breathless and giggly with the fear of being detected. He could not keep his hands off her, and she reveled in the daring and abandon with which he took hold of her breasts or ran his hand up her thigh in public. She noted the salacious or disapproving glances of passersby in the street and wondered what her parents would think of her if they could see her now.

For two weeks they spent every day together, careering

172

about on his motorcycle, swimming, dancing, bowling, playing ball—which he did while she watched—embracing, kissing, and, wherever they could find a feasible place and time for it, making love. Several times she attempted to tell him about herself but gave up in the face of his polite abstracted stare. When she brought up the subject of their relationship, he would say, in the tone of one reciting a catechism, "I love you, I love you," and throw himself upon her.

She did not, however, like his friends. After her college associations of the previous two years, they seemed to her very dull and boorish. They talked about sex incessantly and made juvenile jokes about it. Toward her they were rather leering and presumptuous. Their own girlfriends she found coarse and yet at the same time quite prissy, and they spoke to her always with a faint tone of hostility. Then one evening at a party her young man got drunk on beer, and for the benefit of his onlooking friends, began to paw and talk dirty to her. When she resisted and reproached him, he grew obstreperous and poured out abuse of a kind she had never heard in her life. He called her a tramp and a whore and a pig, asked her who she thought she was, and made as if to force her head between his knees. As she fled to a taxi, she swore a solemn oath never again to be taken in by what might look like sexiness but was really sickness. It took days for the feeling of degradation to wear off.

This little interlude made the prospect of going off to college seem all the more desirable. She had done well in school and had been admitted to a highly regarded small university in the East. One of the things that had added to her own regard for the university—and ostensibly to that of her mother and father as well—was that its living arrangements for students were no longer sexually segregated. Only a year or two earlier, the students had demanded

173

that men and women be allowed to share dormitories, and their demand had been granted. Girls were now ensconced in what had been the men's dorms and vice versa, and even more important to the students' desire that they be treated like free and independent grown people, the college no longer took responsibility for regulating their conduct outside the classroom. Their hours were to be their own, their whereabouts at any given point in time were left entirely up to them.

The world, of course, had done a certain amount of sniggering about this—no doubt fancying, she thought, as even her own parents had not been able to get over doing, that boys and girls left without strict regulation would throw themselves into a kind of perpetual sexual orgy. Whereas all they sought was the power to manage their own affairs and, if anything, precisely to transcend the nasty Victorian dirty-minded attitudes that forced males and females into separate realms of existence lest they be sunk in the swamps of unmanageable erotic fantasy. She, and all her contemporaries, had grown up on a different set of premises about relations between the sexes: that they were healthy, natural, ordinary, that life was not a perpetual sexual temptation or battle, that boys and girls and men and women shared the world in a relaxed and intimate and purely human way. In such a set of premises, sex was kept to its proper, *i.e.,* incidental and health-enhancing, place. Unlike the soul-sickened generations before them, they would be able to live together naturally, sharing, along with classrooms, their living quarters, sleeping quarters, toilet and lounging facilities as, simply, people.

She was given a room to share with another young woman who seemed to her eminently pleasant and agreeable— within a few hours they were trading both clothes and confidences—and down at the far end of the corridor she made the acquaintance of a group of young men who treated her, especially by comparison with her most recent lover and his friends, with great courtesy. The newness of the place, of her classes and daily routine and general social milieu, and especially the predictable nervousness she felt about getting settled in there, put the whole question of sex out of her mind for a while. Within a couple of months, however, she found herself in a slightly inconvenient and uncomfortable situation. Her roommate—by now they were fast friends—was in love with a young man attending school in a college about a hundred miles away. He visited every chance he could get, sometimes hopping a ride in the car of a classmate who was also interested in a girl in this school, sometimes hitchhiking. Having a limited supply of money in his pocket, he was required to spend the night in the room of his young lady. Once or twice the three of them stayed together, but this arrangement proved to be unsatisfactory for everyone. Subsequently, each time he arrived, the girl was forced to seek out an empty bed in someone else's room. This turned out to be chancy as well as disturbing to her study and ordinary nightly routine. One night, for instance, she found herself wandering up and down the corridor in her bathrobe, books and papers under her arm, cigarettes and toothbrush in her hand, knocking on doors with no success until one of the young men in another wing of the dormitory gallantly offered to roll himself in a blanket on the floor and give her his bed. She awoke in the morning with stiff and aching limbs to find him, still wrapped in his blanket, lying alongside her on the spindly cot: the floor had been too cold. It did not occur to her that there was anything remiss in her roommate's conduct, for she would have done the same thing. But she began to dread the prospect of these visitations from the homeless lover and to long for her friend to take up with a young man from this school with a room of his own where they might carry on their dalliances.

She herself, while she was spending a good deal of time in the company of this and that young man, had not as yet come upon any new and special love. Her experiences had put a slight crimp in her inclination to trust the pleasures of intense involvement. Not that she resisted the idea of falling in love again—she was in fact rather looking forward to it; but she had no intention of spending her emotional substance on someone who might, once again, turn out in some way to be unworthy of her trouble. And she was in something of a quandary about what to do with the question of sex as such. Her physical relations with the males in her immediate vicinity were in all other respects perfectly casual and informal. She went about the halls of the dorm in her slip and felt no acute embarrassment at being encountered by her male dormmates. She and her roommate and all their friends and acquaintances in the school thought nothing of holding impromptu mixed gatherings in their rooms at which they might be clad in pajamas or nightgowns, hair in rollers, faces creamed, and manners entirely familial. It did not even occur to them, nor did it appear to occur to the young men either, to associate any of this informality with sexual provocation. Yet she discovered that, for her at least, it was connected in a negative way. For she somehow could not find any of the sharers in this casual behavior attractive to her. They were nice boys, many of them, and sweet boys. Some of them, to be sure, were appealing, some were unprepossessing, and some plainly pathetic, but none, she was indeed surprised to note, struck her as even remotely a candidate for her serious attentions.

On the other hand, the very closeness of the quarters in

which they all lived together, the very easiness of their intermingled life, made the problem of sexual resistance a knotty one to her. If she were truly fond of a young man, and if on some occasion he were to show himself truly in the grip of a need for her—as did in fact happen on several occasions—how delicate and complicated, what a chore and a nuisance, it became to turn him down. She was required to explain herself for hours on end through the routine of a tiresome, circular, and remarkably predictable conversation, a conversation in which she would be coaxed, cajoled, challenged, and usually, in the end, insulted. All she got for her pains was the souring of a friendship. Now and then, mostly to save herself trouble, she would not refuse but resign herself, with a certain inward sigh, to falling into bed. That, however, created problems of its own. For then, on the morning after, she would be required to engage in yet another kind of tiresome and equally predictable conversation. Either, depending on the vanity and uncertainty of her partner, she would be pressed into discoursing on the relative merits of the pleasures he had just afforded her or she would be treated to a hasty, emphatic statement on his part about how she must not now expect that he belonged to her since he was unprepared to make such commitments or he had another girlfriend, or something of the like. No matter what she did under these circumstances, then—sleep with them or not sleep with them—she was somehow left with the feeling that she had been besmirched.

Long before the school year was over, therefore, she came to feel it essential to her peace of mind and good temper, not to mention her studies, that she find a way of moving out of the dorm. Though as a freshman she was not entitled, by one of the few remaining rules of the university, to do so, other freshman girls of her acquaintance had already found some unofficial means of moving into private living quarters. They moved without formal notification or sanction into off-campus apartments being shared by upperclassmen or they set up housekeeping, as she had done so briefly that summer at home with her lover, in the rooms of their boyfriends. Her very determination to find a new way to live, even before she happened on any specific arrangement for it, cheered her considerably and helped her to reestablish a cool equilibrium.

It was at that point that she found a young man with whom she determined to settle down for a while. She met him in a class and was immediately drawn to his air of refinement and gentleness. He was intelligent, dreamy, sensitive, he moved about with a languid grace she thought beautiful, and she had never in her life been so at ease about disclosing all the secrets of her mind and heart as she was with him. She told him everything about herself, the story of her entire life, what she liked, what she feared, what were her characteristic emotions. She told him about her lovers, about her irritation with, and finally alienation from, her parents for their ill-concealed dirty imaginings. He listened as no one had ever listened, his face a tender pool of comprehension and sympathy, and he responded in kind. He too was alienated from his parents, who were brutal, particularly his father, in their disappointment with him. He told her of his psychoanalyst, of the fact that he was presently having deep difficulty concentrating his mind on his studies, of his longing to be loved for simply what he was. Not very long after they met, they sat together on a grassy hillside beneath a cloudless sky and exchanged avowals of profound love. He held her hand, caressing her fingers one by one, while they discussed the details of moving in together.

Of physical sex there had been none between them, not

a hint or gesture. They spoke of sex, though, and were astonished by how much their separate lives so far had brought their minds into agreement. Because of the routine, mechanical way most people expected it to happen, sex was rarely allowed to grow out of, to follow from, any feeling. It had become not an expression of love but only a kind of material precondition for it. That was why people seeking love had imagined they were primarily seeking sex and had turned one of the natural beauties of life into something so frequently tawdry. He spoke to her at length, bringing the words out slowly as if against a terrible and exhausting inner resistance, of his hatred for the heedless, faceless, unfeeling exercise that sexual intercourse appeared to him to be for most men and women. She could barely restrain tears, so moved and illuminated did he leave her. She herself had never been able to put this feeling into words. She had never imagined it possible that a man could share it—more than share it, give it eloquent expression. She cringed to think of the mutual masturbation that had been the sum of her experience with her first lover, of the empty gymnastics with the odious motorcyclist, of the merely socially convenient gropings in the dormitory.

She would settle in his apartment, then, and they would live as the dearest of friends. They would give to one another and take from one another all the human riches they both felt such a great power to bestow and had been forced to keep buried beneath the heartless transactions of mere screwing. When sex had genuinely grown and ripened between them, they would, with pure and unsullied joy, simply give way to it. She could not wait to pack her things.

As they had imagined they would, they got along very well. Sleeping in separate beds created an odd courtesy be-

179

tween them. They tried not to disturb one another at study and became artful at thinking up pleasant diversions for one another at play. He treated her with a gallantry that was as delightful to her as it was utterly unaccustomed. He brought her a single red rose for each weekly anniversary of their having met, for instance, and made a most elaborate and charming surprise party for her birthday. She on her side kept the apartment clean and tidy to a degree entirely uncharacteristic of her, and undertook to keep herself presentable and attractive at all times, from the moment of getting up in the morning till the moment of going to bed. Though at times it made her slightly anxious, the lack of physical intimacy was in the end, she thought, a great spur to all those other and far more important kinds of mutual consideration. Of course, they quarreled now and then. By temperament languorous, he could sometimes become rather edgy and restless. He had infinite patience and understanding for her truest and profoundest weaknesses—nothing more quickly brought a compliment to his lips than an expression on her part of serious self-deprecation—but, she noticed, he could be most intolerant of her small ones. He did not like her eating habits, which were irregular and haphazard, and the sight of her unwashed clothing left somewhere in full view could put him into an ugly temper. He was helpful with the housework but had a way of getting vague, which irritated her, when any major practical decisions had to be made. So they quarreled, but always quietly, talking and unburdening their minds and reaching the point of reconciliation without any betrayal of hatred. He was vague, too, about the summer, about what was to become of them once the school year was over. He mentioned going to Europe, or staying on at the college where he could be near his therapist, but left it entirely unclear as to whether these plans included her. Something—she was not to know until later that it had once again been her instinct responding well in advance of her mind—kept her from pressing the issue. But the uncertainty frequently put her slightly off her mood.

The ripening of sex for which they had agreed to wait did not come. She was content, for no sexual relationship had ever come near to bringing her the sense of love and kindness and fellowship she was enjoying now. Only she found she was beginning to suffer from a curious kind of insomnia. She would wake in the wee hours of the morning with the feeling that she had been in the midst of a heated debate with someone and would spend the hours until daylight tossing restlessly and feeling a pinch of resentment and loneliness that he was sleeping in peaceful oblivion nearby. She also found herself with a terrible and ever-growing need for reassurance. She worried about what she wore and how she looked, a worry she had never sharply experienced before, about whether people liked her, about whether her professors were taking her proper measure. He was unstinting in his reassurances, but strangely enough, the more he reassured her, the more reassurance she felt she needed. Once, for no apparent reason, she spent the entire night sobbing in his arms. He stroked her hair and murmured to her until, exhausted, she fell asleep and slept through the day. After that there was a certain wariness in his eyes, but it never happened again. They did not talk about sex, never even mentioned the word.

Then came the fateful day when she walked in on him unexpectedly. She had been visiting at home over a long weekend and had returned early in order to surprise him. There, in the sudden, hectic disarray of the apartment—empty whiskey bottle, dirty glasses, clothes left strewn where they had been thrown off—she saw in a flash the mystery she had not dared face at the center of her existence. Her beloved friend lay sleeping in a warm tangle of arms and legs, and she actually knew the boy who lay there with him. He was a friend who had sometimes hung around the place and used to beguile them with his witty stories about his professors and every once in a while cook them an elaborate meal. She was clutched by two sensations simultaneously. One was the choking rage of jealousy and the other was a flash of total comprehension: she had, somewhere in her, known it all along. Bits and pieces of conversation, little gestures, delicate and fleeting as snowflakes, seconds of laughter whose tone and purpose were to exclude her, all came flooding back to her memory in a single coherent picture. This was no accidental or circumstantial encounter; it had been going on who knew how long.

The following days were spent in a kind of nonstop marathon of reproach, apology, explanation, promise, and reproach again. Beneath his display of remorse at having hurt and shocked her, she could see that her friend was relieved. He spoke to her with a new detachment—with something that was almost, but not quite, defiance—and though he professed unhappiness, he did so in a voice that carried a new tone of cheer. She on her side was not, she wanted him to know, put off or repelled in any way by the fact that he was a homosexual. She was not so pinched, so feeble, so hung-up, as to imagine that there was only one way to sexual fulfillment. She understood the calculus of love and bodily pleasure and was far beyond making any judgment of what might or might not be included in it. But the betrayal of their friendship, the lack of trust involved in his pretending to total intimacy with her while at the same time making a secret of the major, the central

182

fact of his existence, this had shaken her, she felt, past all recovery. Had he but told her what was truly in his heart, instead of all that garbage about waiting for sex authentically to happen, she would have regarded it as the highest offering of his love and trust. The three of them might even have lived together. She might—who knows—have learned a precious, necessary truth about life and love and men and women. She was prepared to believe that she might have. For among the paradoxes of these terrible days in her life it must be said that not only was his remorse being balanced by a sense of relief but her misery, too, had its balancing emotion: beneath the anguish of feeling betrayed, she was experiencing a certain thrill at being faced with such a deep and arcane sexual complexity. This time, if they knew, her parents *would* be shocked, and unable to follow her into a realm of sexual behavior that would seem inconceivable to them.

Nevertheless, where she least deserved it, she had been subject to his hostility. They had, after long and sleepless days and nights, reached a weary, dispirited reconciliation; he had announced his amazement and gratitude at her tolerance, and she had forgiven him for having sold her short. But she knew that her days in his apartment were numbered. She stayed on, because it was out of the question for her to return to the dormitory, but she spent as little time as possible at home.

That was how she came to meet the group of young women who were to release her from what she had not till then known was her lifelong trap. Because of her need to occupy herself away from the apartment, she began to fling herself into the life of the college community. There was a great bustle, she discovered, going on all around her. Meetings, demonstrations, lectures were being held every day to protest one or another of the several outrages being committed by society. She had all along been in sympathy with such protesting, having received the beginning of an education in the prevailing evils of America at the hands of her first lover and his friends, but she had somehow been too caught up in private questions to take an active part. Now she was starting to take notice of the larger world. And one night, happening into a meeting called by a campus women's group—there was to be a speaker, it had been announced, addressing herself to the topic, "How to Beat the Bum Sex Rap"—she had for the first time really taken hold of the idea that her difficulties with young men over the past two or three years had not in the least been of her own, or even necessarily of their, making. Unlike what she had imagined, relations between the sexes were far from a merely private individual matter. This idea had come to her before, but only in a scattered, fleeting way, when she had been hurt or angry or felt herself somehow to have been treated unfairly. It had not seriously occurred to her, when she was humbling herself with her first lover, and humiliating herself with her second, or defending herself in the dorm, or allowing herself to be so bitterly deceived by her homosexual friend, that she had been caught up in nothing less than a major, perhaps a decisive, social issue.

Thus, the night of that meeting she felt as if her whole life were being suddenly stripped down to its essentials, as if a great artificial structure put up between her actual nature and her conduct as a social being were being demolished by a swing of the wrecker's ball.

She had attended the meeting because she had been feeling sorely of late that for her sex was indeed turning out to be a bum rap of some kind. But she had not put the pieces of her own problems and those of her friends together into a full picture of the necessary and inevitable

lot of women—a lot, as the speaker said, which cried out
for protest and action far ahead of all those other worthy
causes which as students they had been called upon to support. The nub of the matter, the speaker told the audience—she was a writer and philosopher of growing eminence, much touted in literary circles and by her publisher
and yet, the girl thought wonderingly, able to express herself in the simplest and most graphic of terms—the nub of
the matter was something they called the sexual revolution. Women had for going on ten thousand years been
exploited by men, robbed of their sexual essence in order
that they might be turned into homemakers and breeders,
twisted and turned by a dozen different ideologies, from
religious taboo to capitalist-inspired belief in consumption,
to keep them submissive beneath the yoke of heterosexual
monogamy. And the greatest hoax of all that had been
played on them was the modern idea of sexual freedom.
In the name of this so-called "revolution," a revolution—
and here the speaker fairly whinnied—purporting to be
on women's behalf, they had at last been robbed of the one
small spark of humanity that had still remained to them
through all previous systems of exploitation. They had for
one thing been sent off in pursuit of the vaginal orgasm—a
thing, it was now being scientifically proved, that did not
even exist—in order that to all their other feelings of in-
sufficiency and dependence before the power of male aggression they might now take on the feeling of sexual failure. How many members of the audience had not pretended to be having an orgasm in order to forestall the
charge of failure and frigidity? Why had they done this?
Because, unknown to themselves, they had been enlisted
in the service of the male ego. (Here, the young woman
felt as if her heart were leaping through her ribcage and
her temples began to pound.) For another thing, the

185

speaker went on, they had been set "free" to make themselves and their bodies available to the lusts of each and every passing man. They had been told they no longer had to wait for marriage to become sexually active, and had thereby provided men with a vast supply of sexual playthings for which these men didn't even have to pay the minimal former price of providing a roof over a woman's head and food for her mouth. In the name of "freedom," they had been pressed into cutthroat competition with their unhappy sisters, the hookers. They had been sold into a kind of slavery that even the lowliest harem-dweller, for all her beastlike misery, had not been forced to endure. It had taken men, who were after all none too bright, millennia to hit upon this simplest and most effective scheme for ordering life entirely to their convenience. The real sexual freedom of women was something men had from nearly the beginning of time been terrified to face, for women in their natural sexual state were too powerful. Indeed, given the fact that it was the clitoris, rather than the penis, which was the true instrument of female pleasure, men had glimpsed the truth that they were not sexually necessary to women at all. And they had hastened to create a society in which women would be too burdened and oppressed even to remember, let alone demand, what such a thing as freedom would truly mean to them.

By the time the speaker had finished, the young woman felt drunk. She wanted to laugh and she wanted to weep at the same time. Everything she heard had in one sense sounded new and startling to her and yet was in another sense as familiar, as foreknown, as the circulation of her blood. What made an even greater impression on her than the speaker's formulations was the fact that she had been listening to them in the midst of a whole group of other young women who were evidently responding to them as she was. Finally, she thought, and for the first time, she understood the meaning of the word "solidarity."

Leaving the meeting room, she ran into a girl whom she had known slightly in the dorm. She had not at the time been much attracted to this girl, finding her rather crude and aggressive and pathetically (she had thought then) committed to denying her personal charm. Tonight the girl greeted her warmly, invited her for coffee with a group who had come to the meeting together, and she was grateful. They talked into the wee hours—she ended up spending the night on the floor in the room of one of her newfound friends—and the next day and the next day after that. They told one another the stories of their sexual careers; some of the stories were exactly like her own, some were much much worse. She had not known she could feel so angry. When it came her turn to tell her tale, she heard herself saying things she had never said to anyone before, and she remembered things—slights, insults, her own fearful and fawning responses to them—that she was not even aware had registered themselves on her mind. How much more amazed she was, then, to find her interlocutors merely nodding in recognition as if everything bad that had happened to her in the course of her entire life had been perfectly ordinary and predictable.

These girls had organized themselves into a group. There was no escaping their degrading exploitation as individuals, they told her; the whole of society was mobilized against them. Only a revolution into a society organized to make no effective distinctions between the sexes would free them from their false and powerless condition. Here she found that many of the things being said to her—particularly by the aggressive and unprepossessing young woman (whom she now, on close inspection, regarded as having her own kind of beauty)—interested her less. Sta-

187

LIBERAL PARENTS, RADICAL CHILDREN

tistics of oppression, talk about institutions and large social arrangements, were something she had never been able to give her mind to. She was certain that what her new companions said on these matters was true, and she was content to support them, but what really moved her was the idea of how she herself and all her friends had been taken in and badly used. If nothing less than a revolution were necessary to alter the conditions that had so enslaved her to the sexual needs and demands of all the boys she knew, so be it. But she was frank to admit to herself that for the time being anyway it was those conditions foremost that held her attention. During their discussions, it was she who managed each time to bring the conversation back to the point where they could resume their exchange of private stories.

For themselves, the group decided, there was immediate remedy. Real revolutions were made in any case not by those who sought to constitute themselves a new government but by those who had the courage to live in accordance with their convictions. They would find a house and live in it together and urge others to join them, withdrawing from all but the most unavoidable contact with men. Some day, perhaps, when they had freed themselves from every last impulse to submission, when they had found their own authentic sexual nature as women, when they had set their minds, bodies, and spirits to live only as that nature required, they might return, now as full and self-knowing autonomous individuals, to the company of men.

When school was out, she returned home to tell her parents of her new plans. She was by now a thoroughly assimilated member of her group and well acquainted with its entire line of reasoning. She had read a sheaf of mani-

188

festos, mimeographed articles, poems, and three or four books, all devoted to the subject of the sexual exploitation of women. She herself had written an article, a bitter dissection of her summertime affair with the young man on the motorcycle, which was to appear in a collection of writings put out by an organization of radical women. So she was able succinctly and with authority to set before her mother and father the plan to create a women's commune.

Her parents had been aware that something new and interesting was going on among a number of young women at colleges like their daughter's—something related to student demands for a better, more just world in general but not quite the same form of rebellion as they had grown accustomed to—and they had been a bit confused about it. They could not quite understand, from the newspaper reports they had been reading, whether the girls were insisting on the right to the kind of sexual freedom their daughter already enjoyed or whether, as sometimes seemed to be the case, they were claiming such freedom not to be enough.

Nothing they had read prepared them for her appearance and manner. Looking at her now, severe, earnest, legs unshaven, nails clipped to the quick, talking rapidly and in some new alien rhetoric, they realized that for the first time in their lives they had failed to receive the message of a new movement of protest. Her father snorted several times during her account of the sexual oppression of women; two red spots of rage stood out on his cheekbones. But truth to tell, he was, as he inwardly admitted, what they called conflicted. Some part of him felt an instantaneous empathy with all modern men who had disciplined themselves for the delicate task of ministering to the pleasure of their women and would now be faced with the discovery that they had all along been regarded as nothing more than exploitive beasts. He glanced at his wife, anxiously wondering how she was responding to the things his daughter was saying. Some other part of him, however, felt soothed by the idea that all his daughter's sexual cavortings, some of which he had been forced to witness with a show of good grace, had quite obviously brought her no pleasure. The idea of a women's commune made Everyman in him uneasy, but it brought the father in him a curious kind of relief. Torn in this way, he said very little.

But the mother was simply stunned to hear her daughter's outpourings. She had been so taken up with the idea that her daughter no longer had to pretend to purity—either before her parents or before society itself—as she herself had once had to do, that the possibility of the girl's disaffection in matters sexual had not even crossed her mind. She had supposed her daughter to be healthy and well-adjusted, sexually responsive and well in charge of herself: had not her therapist pointed out to her years ago that the inhibitions imposed by being a "nice" girl, coupled with the need to deceive and dissemble, were what had been standing in the way of her own sexual health and fulfillment? Now her daughter was announcing that the very opportunity afforded her to behave openly and easily about sex was precisely the bitterest of all her oppressions. The mother demanded that her daughter explain more clearly the nature of her complaint.

When they were alone together, the girl covered the ground once more, this time with a gentleness and patience her mother had never seen in her before. She had come to appreciate her mother, and all mothers, for the first time, the girl said. For she could see for the first time how much of everything that she had once found irritating in their relationship with one another had been merely the

190

result of her mother's own victimization as a woman. They were in fact not mother and daughter to her anymore, but sisters, suffering from a common historical exploitation at the hands of men and bound together by their common designation as the wretched of the earth. In the process of coming to her new consciousness, she had remembered all sorts scenes from her childhood, scenes which she had paid no attention to at the time, as little children don't, but which had flooded in upon her as soon as she began to think of her mother under the aspect of eternal womanhood. There was a time when she had witnessed an argument between her parents, in which her mother had been unquestionably right but, cowering in fear before her husband's masculine passion—carrying, as does all masculine passion, the implicit threat that having had his way with her he was prepared to leave her—the mother had submitted and apologized. There was a time when, in response to her mother's complaint that she felt bored and overburdened and imprisoned in the house, she had heard her father (during this conversation, the young woman had slipped into referring to him as "that man"), with an unpleasant laugh, issue the reply, "Who the hell told you to have children?" *Who the hell told you to have children?* The girl, the veins in her neck purple and swollen, was practically beside herself. As if—she spat the words—there was no connection whatever between his so-called manly urges and the having of children. Well, she could see it all now: women pregnant, burdened with children, feeling themselves dependent, trying to please, to placate, pleading with their lords and masters under the illusion that they needed them, when all the while they were only being kept chained and cowed so that they might render service.

It was too late for her mother now, the daughter sighed, but she regarded herself as setting out to make things

191

right for both their sakes and for the sake of every woman who had ever been forced to live her life according to the principle of pleasing men. She had liberated herself from all the artifices women use to rouse the male mating instinct. She was well along in the course of liberating her mind from all its remaining vestiges of female passiveness and concern for male approval. And together with her new circle of comrades, she was on the way to creating an atmosphere in which women might come to themselves, learn to find, and assert, and base their future lives upon, their very own demands.

The mother was strangely stirred by the spectacle of this extraordinary being she had given birth to. Her daughter's newfound tenderness toward her was, to be sure, very much part of her being stirred, but she had always expected that sooner or later they would become good friends. Moreover, she was disquieted by the idea of a women's commune. She could not summon the nerve to say it—she had so often in the past few years suffered the accusation of dirty-mindedness—but such an arrangement as her daughter had outlined smacked to her of lesbianism. Be that as it may, however, she found herself reverberating, almost against her will, to the girl's ideas. Yes, she knew what these young women were talking about. She thought of her own girlhood humiliations, of a time she had, after his ardent pressure, surrendered to a young beau only to find that when he had finished with his transport he was not grateful or loving to her but for some unfathomable reason annoyed. She thought of a year spent in anxious determination, on the couch and in her own bed, striving, striving, mostly, she now realized, to satisfy her husband's egotistical wish to account himself a successful lover. She *had* been saddled with the children, she *had* been imprisoned in the house, she *had* worried, particularly in latter years, about whether or not her husband was still truly pleased with her while it had not even occurred to her to question whether he still truly pleased her. And for all the principled overcoming of inbred reactions it had entailed, by casting her daughter so young into the terrible sea of sex she had not genuinely freed her but only disarmed her for the long battle with men.

Perhaps, though, she consoled herself, she had had something of a hand in freeing her daughter after all, because these young women had taken advantage of their plentiful sexual experience to learn something about freedom that she for one had never imagined. It was a time in general, she thought happily, for adults to learn from their children instead of the other way around. She did not say any of this to her husband—for her daughter had been right, it was too late for her, at least with regard to the fixed essentials of her marriage. But, in private, she embraced her daughter tearfully and offered up a silent prayer for her success.

FIVE

The Communard

Had his world not promised to be a rather different place from the one they themselves had grown up in, they might have been extremely worried for their son. He was so sweet and gentle. There was not to be discerned in him a single drop of the kind of harshness or aggression that had once been thought necessary to the successful completion of the masculine character. All the fierce drive with which as a very little boy he had rollicked through the household had been tamed to some inner, higher purpose, had got relocated, as it were, from his limbs to the secret places of his soul. Not that he was a namby-pamby—what would in the crude desperation of the streets in their own childhoods have been called a sissy. On the contrary, in accordance with the deeper, wiser notion of such things in currency now, he was a most manly boy. He could be very firm, when something important or truly desirable to him was at stake. And he could be indignant, which indeed he often passionately was. Nevertheless, it was quite incon-

197

ceivable of him that he could be involved in violence of any kind. One simply could not imagine his pushing, pounding, scheming, racing anyone for anything, or offering a gratuitous cruelty. Nor would one imagine his shoving people aside and forcing his way. When he was being firm, it was usually with respect to a wish of his own that had little bearing on others, and when he was being indignant, it was always with respect to something that had outraged his peculiarly pulsating sense of justice. For the rest, he was almost incredibly tender. Since the onset of adolescence, when he began to bury the remaining traces of childish turmoil, he had barely even raised his voice.

There had of course been signs of this in him all along. As a small child, whenever he had been injured or done down in some way by one of his fellows, he had responded by weeping bitterly—more in shock and disappointment at the discovery that life held arbitrary suffering, his parents felt, than over the particular injury at hand—but he had rarely engaged in any form of retaliation. He had taken whatever comfort was to be had from his mother's repeated assertion that the little boy or little girl who had done ill by him was to be accounted far more unhappy, at bottom, than he. He had always hung back from playing games where there were winners and losers, finding it difficult to understand why an activity whose end was supposed to be the pleasure and entertainment of its participants should carry the built-in necessity of hurt feelings. And for the same reason, he had resisted taking part in competitions. Invidiousness of any kind had from the very first struck him as a form of outright cruelty to people. He himself, for example, showed a gift for drawing; sketches and cartoons dashed off by him dotted the walls of his house and elicited admiring comments from all visitors; but when one of his teachers had informed him that she meant to enter a couple of pieces of his work in a school contest, he had put away his crayons and papers for several years.

Most of all, however, the quality of tenderness—of quickened response to the possibility of hurt and suffering and determination to set all such possibility aside—had revealed itself to them in his relation to the issue of property. Never had they known a child to be so uncaring, so easy and heedless and uncalculating, about the entire business of possession. Laughing, they called him their aristocrat, but behind their laughter lay a very real wonder and humility. There was nothing he owned, with the possible exception of a ragged stuffed animal or two, that he would not after the first day's gusto for its newness happily hand off to a playmate. Be it a book, a game, a toy, or even, as was the case in the week following his eighth birthday, a brand new wristwatch, he had no more notion of keeping it safe and exclusive to himself than he would have had had it been an extra piece of penny candy. He would not dream of refusing, or disappointing, any expressed desire to share with him in his worldly goods. By the same token, he was utterly bewildered by anyone else's refusal to share on exactly the same basis with him. More than once they had noticed the uncomprehending stare with which he evinced his puzzlement as some angry child snatched a belonging from his hands. All things were quite obviously, in his view, there for the common use, convenience, and pleasure of all people. Now and then, for the sake of social peace they were forced to admonish him not to lay hands on objects that did not belong to him. It sickened them to do this, for they knew how genuinely little he understood or credited the sanctity of property and how few rights in it he on his side ever wished to claim for himself. Nor was his attitude to money in any essential way different. Whatever money was given to him—and, with the presence in his life of doting grandparents and relatives, he was sometimes in possession of what were, for his age, fairly hefty sums—was quickly spent, a major part of it on his friends or even strangers who happened by. If there were coins in his pocket at the time, no charity collection box, no panhandler, blind beggar, or rummy seeking "coffee," was ever passed by.

They must, they were sure, have indicated to him by the looks on their faces and the tones of their voices how much they approved of such generosity and concern for others; but clearly the habit of unselfishness went far deeper into the wellsprings of his personality than any mere wish to bask for a moment in parental approval. All of it together—his gentleness, lack of violence, detestation of competition, unconcern for his possessions, incapacity to horde his money—spelled out the dynamics of a noble and loving nature. Any small annoyance they felt with him (for naturally, his easy indifference to property and money included their property and money as well) paled to less than nothing beside the recognition of his extraordinary, and extraordinarily precocious, spiritual gifts.

Such gifts, they believed, had at least in part to be a happy accident, a coming together of the right fundamental endowments with the right enabling circumstances. They lived after all very much as others lived and tried to bring up their son by pretty much the same set of precepts. And yet all around them they could see children and young people dedicated in ways that were only too familiar to them to the process of grasping advantages wherever and over whomever they could. Thus it seemed reasonable to them that something open and giving had been fixed in the boy's personality very early in his life, if not indeed in the womb. That this something had required the proper set of opportunities to come to full flower was only com-

200

mon sense. Had they for instance subjected him to cruelty of any kind, he would surely have learned the ways of cruelty. Had they pinched him with privations, he would no doubt have grown up with a far meaner spirit. Had they dealt with him violently, he would have had no model of behavior for his impulse of gentleness—the impulse itself would very likely have died aborning. Had they sought to measure and value each of his attainments only by a standard of comparison with others, he would have been incapable, at least for years and years, of identifying the hurt that follows from comparison. And they had to admit, though by itself they regarded this as a minor and trivial point, that had they been less economically secure, some element of their own worry about money might have escaped into the atmosphere and put a crimp or damper to his largesse.

As it happened, they had never knowingly been cruel to him and never violent. Even in their worst states of annoyance or aggrievement with something he had done, they tried to keep in mind that they had the power to wound him far more than he to wound them, and to tread carefully lest some uncontrolled display of their emotions have deeper consequences than they intended. They had slapped him occasionally but only by the dictates of policy, having decided to reserve this extreme and unaccustomed measure for situations involving some danger to him. When he was very little, they slapped him for stepping into the street or playing with the electrical outlets. Once he was given a rather severe spanking for having climbed onto the sill of an open and unscreened window, and later, he was given the same treatment when they caught him experimenting with the idea of setting fire to a pile of papers in his room. On each of these occasions, as soon as he appeared in no uncertain terms to have received their message, they hastened to take him in their arms and console him so that he should understand there was nothing personal in their anger.

Nor did they set artificial standards for his achievements. They tried to communicate to him all the time—and judging by the results, seemed to have done so very well—that everything he did was for its own, and his own, sake. They never indicated to him that he was to master anything, or excel at anything, either because they required it of him or because it would in some way make him better than others. When he learned to read, and they would have been less than human had they been unaware that he did so at a comparatively early age, they urged him on only in terms of the enormous pleasure reading would one day bring him. When he began to draw, and they would have been less than human had they failed to take note that his work was far advanced of that of his contemporaries, they refused to spoil his joy in what he was doing by making him conscious of the vast discipline it would one day be his to conquer. And so it was with each new attainment. Having vividly in mind the days of their their own childhood, when even the slightest display of gift or interest was immediately translated by parental greed into some potentially exploitable future purpose, they took care to make him know that their delight in his achievements was a delight *for* him, not simply *in* him for the promise of distinction he held out to themselves. Not the least of their teachings against greed, they made so bold as to believe, lay in their own evident lack of greediness about his obligation to make them proud of him.

And above all, they realized, they had enabled him to fulfill his own tendency toward generosity and selflessness by their behavior with respect to mere material things. They were not rich, at least not as that condition is reckoned by the really rich themselves, but they had, somewhat to their surprise, reached a point of prosperity where they need not feel that money was any sort of an issue except on the very highest levels. Certainly as far as the upbringing, education, and entertainment of their child was concerned, they could not imagine ever being faced with the decision that he would have to be deprived of anything he seriously wanted. This fact was not, of course, by itself so important: neither of them had grown up poor, and yet they had been brought up—as they were to discover only in adult life, far in excess of what had been dictated by the financial condition of their respective families—in the morality of self-denial. Somehow it had been considered "good" for one, good for one's character and grasp of life, to be left in a kind of steady state of yearning and wanting and wishing. The obverse consequence of this idea, only on the surface was it an ironic one, was that things of this world purchasable with money took on an abiding, indeed an overriding, significance in the calculus of human happiness. It had taken them years of catching up on their unsated youthful appetites before they had been able to liberate themselves from the idea that there was any basic satisfaction to be had from the accumulation of money and the things money could buy.

Their son was certainly not growing up as they had in this regard. Not so much because they had come to any conscious decision that they would teach him to hold money and things of small account but because they had acted in accordance with their genuine impulses. They saw no reason, on any particular occasion, to deny him what he asked for. No doubt they were moved by old memories of their own disappointments; no doubt somewhere inside them there lurked old resentments at the effort and importance they had been forced to attach to the most commonplace items of childish desire. In any case, they were not only willing but, they found, positively eager, to fill his requests—and grateful that they were in a position to do so without giving it any thought.

His response to all this, as might have been predicted, was an admirable unconcern for his possessions. They lay heaped about his room in a cozy disarray that signaled his perfect ease in assimilating them to his life without the need for any careful inventory or stocktaking. Sometimes, in the determination to create a little space and order, his mother would throw a certain number of them away, and he never even seemed to notice. Money itself, he had grasped with an instinctive sophistication that put him well ahead of even the wisest heads in the nineteenth century, was there to be used. Outside of what it could provide, money was mere garbage, an inhuman abstraction that, if taken seriously, atrophied the best part of the spirit. If they occasionally wished, for his own sake, that he had somehow acquired a more reasoned sense of the connection between money and the future, they knew on the other hand that such a notion was precisely what impelled people to be mean and small in their dealings with others. As it was, he did not dream that money could be withheld from him, and by the same token, he did not dream of withholding his own money from most of the people who might be eligible to ask him for it.

Thus it could be said that in some sense they had taught him to be open and generous—by actual precept as well as by an underlying attitude of refusal to uphold in any way the old morality of self-denial, which was in the end pre-eminently a morality of denying others. But he had also taught *them* something. For whereas beneath their intention to take as little notice as possible of the goods with which they had filled their life there still persisted some traces of their former nervousness about acquisition, his own indifference was genuine and totally without art or thought. He provided for them a model of what real transcendence looked like. Real transcendence was not the transcendence of desire—he wanted something new virtually every day—nor of the passion to possess—he could not rest until a request of his was fulfilled—but of the feeling that what one possessed was of any lasting importance. It was nothing for him to see his belongings destroyed or to give them away. Sometimes when his mother watched him, she felt herself to be the lowliest bourgeois moneygrubber by comparison.

Once, for instance, she bought him a set of oil paints. She had gone to an art-supply store and, thinking to delight him and enhance his life with a surprise introduction to oil-painting, had bought him a full artist's set in a handsome wooden case. The next day, in the company of a group of far from artistic friends, he was to be seen devising games which involved squeezing out blobs of paint onto bits of paper and trampling them with one's heels onto the pieces of the canvas she had also bought for the new enterprise. She had to fight back the impulse to scold or to lecture him on the subject of waste. He was doing with his new possession what his own sense of its possibilities dictated; by what tired and discredited standard of property relations was she entitled to call it waste?

Another time, a new and handsomely equipped bicycle was stolen from him. Instead of having to console him, however, she found that he was consoling her: it was only a bicycle, he said, only after all a construction of a few pieces of metal and rubber; the thief had not injured *him* in any way; probably the boy who stole it needed it more than he; a bike was replaceable—any time they wanted, even that very day, they could just go out and buy a new one. She felt both humbled and chastened by how much better so young a boy was able to deal with the question of material things than she was.

Taken all together, then, these qualities in their son —whatever might, from the point of view of his parents' own momentary convenience, be his shortcomings—promised a kind of new moral and social start for mankind. Having no occasion for envy, and no natural inclination to it, he might grow up without the single most compelling basis for hostility to his fellows. Having no truck with violence, and no taste for it, he might also take part in constituting a more decent and civilized social order. Having no outer need, and clearly no inner pressure, to husband his stock of goods, he might learn to take true possession of the world instead of being possessed by it. To be sure, they harbored no illusions about the potential effect of the boy himself, or even an army like him, on that vast collectivity called Society. Indeed, the society around them if anything appeared to them to be getting worse—more violent, more driven by greed, more indifferent to human suffering—than ever before. But the possibility of creating a pocket of sensitive civility, a kind of island of high moral and spiritual standard in the sea of selfishness and crassness that American society had seemed to them to have become, he offered great hope. Their own home had been such an island as far as they were concerned; now perhaps there would be a community, and one in which the sons might steady and reconfirm and realize fully the aspirations of the fathers.

They did not, to be sure, often think about him in connection with so grand and large an issue as the future of society—especially when he was still a child. In the midst of their daily dealings and inevitable small troubles with him, they continued in an entirely private way to wonder at him and be gratified by him and to puzzle over the question of what would be the end translation, in practical terms, of the very special loveliness of his nature. But though they were for the most part too taken up with the particularities of his character to talk much about it, they were aware that he was living in a world significantly altered from the one in which they had taken their bearings. If American society as a whole had from their point of view grown rather ugly in its piggish intoxication with new found wealth, that unique and blessed corner of American society in which he was privileged to grow up seemed to be in the throes of a kind of spiritual revolution. Some part of the happy influence on him was coming also, to a certain extent anyway, from his surroundings.

The ethic of violence, for example, of an eye for an eye, or, in the parlance of classroom and playground, of "hitting back," was quite as alien to his school and to the streets and backyards and homes where he played as it was to his own home. Disputes among the children were adjudicated by adults, parents, teachers, sometimes even passing strangers, always with appeals to reason and mutual understanding. Each altercation provided a fresh occasion for encouraging the children to discuss and define the course of justice, and was brought, wherever possible, satisfactorily to term by an exchange of apologies accompanied by a heightened appreciation of the feelings of all concerned.

The old principle of competition had been considerably weakened: grades, contests, prizes for academic achievement had pretty much gone by the boards; the children tended to be praised and rewarded far more for effort than for outcome; even at birthday parties the traditional games of skill were generally concluded with the distribution of the same small favors to everyone who had participated. The petty triumphs and real heartbreaks of simple success and failure were being supplanted virtually everywhere in the children's special province by the far more kindly and humanizing standards of performance in relation only to individual capacities.

And finally, there had been the enthronement of the idea of sharing. This had no doubt always been paid lip-service as a nice and virtuous idea—certainly few educators or guardians of children could ever have been so philosophically rebellious as to preach the superiority of plain selfishness. But in their son's world sharing was no longer merely a pretty and harmless ideal; it had become an iron-clad, enforceable rule of conduct. Gone was any of the virtue hitherto attached to the assertion, "This is *mine.*" And gone with it was the whole ancient puritan structure of training and belief created to ensure the sanctity of property: the idea that one worked alone—schoolwork was now conducted in group projects—the idea that one earned the rewards and punishments of one's conduct alone— rewards and punishments were also almost always meted out to groups or classes—and the idea that what belonged to one, in the way of goods or praise or even feelings, was a kind of sacred private trust. These ideas, it was now understood, had been at bottom nothing more than the old-fashioned capitalist property-worshipping methods masked as a religion of private conscience. Sharing was more than a form of primitive Christian kindliness, then; it was a discipline for learning that one's responsibilities as well as one's advantages had always to be engaged with and to implicate others.

Not all the children with whom he shared his spiritually privileged corner of American society, of course, had responded to its prevailing influences as readily as their son had. Certain of his friends and acquaintances appeared to

208

remain bound by a set of values familiar from their own youth. These children continued to strive and battle and hoard their possessions and, the boys among them, to judge themselves by the criteria of that old harsh code of small-time masculine ego-building. But the influence was nevertheless there. His schools, his books, the conversation of the adults with whom he came most closely into contact, even the camps to which he had sometimes been sent to spend the summer, had all more or less reflected a new feeling that the highest virtues for him to attain to were the virtues of gentleness, sociability and the spirit of cooperation.

By the time he reached college, everything they had seen developing in him had come to full flower. He cared very little for his possessions, with the exception of his record player, and even that he fussed over in an uncharacteristic way only for the fact that it brought music, rather than a sense of spreading ownership, into his life. He owned many things, and used them, lent them, or parted with them in a totally casual manner. The father had been impressed, indeed a little overwhelmed, by his relation to the car they had bought him for his high-school graduation gift. The boy thought nothing of making it available to his friends, or of using it for such potentially damaging purposes as hauling furniture, cartons, skiing equipment, or as many as a dozen people at a time; in a year's time, the vehicle had the cozy, used-up look of something very old that had been treated as a mere convenience. The father, remembering both the thrill and leaden sense of responsibility he himself had experienced on the acquisition of his first car—an experience that had not to that day entirely departed from him—and the measures of painstaking care and worry it had led him to, found it almost incomprehensible how the boy could be so masterfully matter-of-fact about so major a species of owning. Like his wife, he too suffered many moments of shame mingled with pride in his son for his new and obviously proper and healthy sang-froid about the world's goods.

The boy cared, if anything, even less about his appearance. He dressed himself, and groomed himself, without the least consideration of all those issues of taste and ascriptive class status that had once, for his parents at his age, made the subject of clothes a sometimes painful one. As with everything else in his life, they had stinted on nothing in the area of clothing and personal equipment. When he was a little child, it had pleased them to see him moving about with perfect ease in the best that money could buy. It meant more than that he was making a showing to the world which would reflect credit on his home and background. It meant that he was growing up taking for granted all those graces, social and sartorial, that they had strained mightily to provide themselves. They were amused, therefore—and also, it must be admitted, sometimes considerably irritated—by the revelation vouchsafed to them in his adolescence that taking such things for granted ultimately meant wishing to divest oneself of them entirely. Both their amusement and their irritation, however, were superficial as compared with their deeper recognition that his appearance contained a sober and important message about himself: his values were such as to preclude any display of economic advantage or personal vanity. No matter how much they wished that he might pay just a tiny bit more attention to the conventional requirements of ordinary propriety, they would be the first to concede that his refusal to do so bespoke his commitment to the higher morality.

The most important evidence that his childhood sweetness and generosity had ripened into being major features of his adult character, though, was to be found in his ideas about society and his own future role in it. He believed as fiercely as he had when he was four years old in the simple categories of fair and not fair. With each new step in the process of his coming to maturity these categories had expanded to include more of the world outside himself until, finally, he was able to apply them pointedly to the institutions, customs, and practices of the entire country and then the entire world. Just as certain things had self-evidently been unfair in the days of those earliest encounters with his own little universe of social action— that some child should have more than another, for instance, or go unpunished for a punishable misdeed or obversely, suffer punishment for something of which he was innocent—so it was now with the affairs of society as a whole. For those with eyes to see, and hearts to feel, and spirits to care, the boy knew, injustices of every kind nakedly revealed themselves. They were injustices of a not very different order from the ones that had outraged his childish innocence, only writ a good deal larger. There were whole groups of people who had been deprived of their rights, their dignity, their share of the world's goods, and even of the hope and energy to make any protest against their treatment. Despite the complex arguments advanced by certain mean-minded sophists—no doubt hired for this very purpose by the oppressors—arguments from history, from politics, from economics, for him it was no more complicated than adding 2 and 2 to determine where the rights and wrongs of a given social situation lay. Nor could anything in the world, as far as he was concerned, take precedence over the need and desire to see that each and every one of these self-evident wrongs and unfairnesses be put to rights.

He spoke to his parents a great deal about all this, never, to their minds miraculously, allowing his passion to overcome his soft-tongued composure. They were not at all surprised to hear him inveighing against poverty, against the abominable condition of black people, against the rapacity and cruelty that permitted women and children to walk around starving in a land of unbelievable plenty, or of the cynicism that deprived young men of a decent chance to realize themselves and then slimily reproached them for being failures. It did not surprise them because it was so naturally a product of the concerned and loving nature they had long ago discerned in him.

How such commitment would actually be translated in his future life neither they nor, as it appeared, he could be quite sure. Through his first two or three years of college, when asked by their friends or relatives about his plans, he would reply that he meant to do something "for others." There was nothing surprising to them in this announcement, neither in its expressed determination to make some direct and palpable contribution to his fellow men nor in its implicit deemphasis of the whole issue of worldly ambition and wealth. That he refused to think of work in terms of private gain was of a piece with everything they most admired in him—his purity of heart and his freedom from that all-consuming love of vainglory which had driven so many of their own contemporaries to offer up their very lives in pursuit of a few paltry baubles of status. They could not deny themselves the satisfaction of feeling that at least some of his freedom was a product of their own teachings and values; for as Americans, the children and grandchildren of anxiety-filled immigrants, they too had taken part—rather successfully, they might say—in the mad scramble for success and money and had understood, in time to release their son from it, just how murderous and destructive that scramble was. And they were grateful to have been in the position to bring the boy up without any pressure from the dread of economic insecurity.

Money that did not liberate one precisely from the crass coarsening preccupation with money was, they had found, perhaps the greatest enslavement of all.

What one did "for others," however, was not the easiest of questions to answer. In terms of the kinds of careers most familiar to them, one could be a doctor, for example, or a social worker or a psychologist or an engineer. None of these careers made much of an appeal to him, and they could not in all honesty say they blamed him. The benefits brought to people by a bold and imaginative engineer could be very great, but they were long-range and indirect benefits, so long-range that they could never satisfy an urge like their son's to touch actual people's lives in a personal way. And at the moment it was nearly impossible to imagine what kind of work an engineer might do that would not sooner or later be pressed into the service of society's more evil impulses, the making of war or furthering the intolerable dehumanizations of technology. Besides, he had never been particularly adept at mathematics or science, finding them too abstract for his kind of intelligence, which was essentially empathetic and emotive. Psychology, then, would have seemed to be a field far more congenial to him; but he could not convince himself—just as they were no longer convinced—that easing the strictly private pain of individuals, who were in any case more likely than not to be middle-class individuals, had much connection with the urgent problems of the people who were nowadays most in need. Besides, the road from where he was to becoming an accredited psychologist would be a dreary obstacle course of irrelevant experimentation, lengthy and demanding and mechanical research, and studies so remote from real people and the societies they lived in that one could, from sheer distraction, be carried far afield from one's original purpose.

Training to be a social worker or a teacher had these disadvantages and even more: far from opening the soul or instructing it in the ways of love and guidance, such training merely deadened. Schools of education and social work were turning out the kind of public bureaucrats who were, in the formulation then currently popular, themselves a central part of the problem rather than architects of the solution. Besides, he had heard unpleasant things about the regimen and training requirements of a postgraduate education in these fields and could not see himself devoting years to the acquisition of something he would then be obliged simply to throw off. Medicine, of course, was quite simply out of the question. In theory, doctors helped people; in practice, they only helped themselves—to heaps upon brutally and for the most part illegitimately gotten heaps of money. There was something else about the study of medicine: it was a form of ensuring that one would be wealthy and respected which had been so ardently urged upon the members of their generation by ignorant and status-hungry parents that it had actually become a kind of intergenerational joke with them. They would no more have dreamed of suggesting to their son that he might one day become a doctor, even in the idleness of playing the old game of "What are you going to be?" when he was a very little boy, than they would have dreamed of giving him a shoeshine box and sending him out on the streets to bring home some contribution to the family finances. Besides, he had always been an unusually squeamish child—probably, they felt, as part of his keen and primitive hatred of violence. In high school, a special arrangement had been made with his biology teacher to have him excused from assignments involving dissection.

They knew that such a list of careers was in itself a symptom of their own limited and tradition-bound perception of the world's work. No doubt there were hundreds of

214

different ways in which a young man might express his concern for an involvement in the condition of his fellow men. The very revolution in standards which had made it possible for their son to be gentle without shame must also have broadened, far beyond their own narrow ken, the possibilities for incorporating his extraordinary values at, so to speak, the work-place.

The trouble was that, for the time being anyway, he had so little margin for the slow but necessary process of finding himself in the world. He himself had frequently questioned the value of his remaining in school at all, because it seemed to him so poignantly a waste of time to be fooling around with books and papers and examinations whose main purpose was to fit him for becoming part of the system it was his highest ambition to avoid. Under normal circumstances, they would have advised him to take time off and look around him a bit—travel around the world, say, or try his hand on an amateur basis at one thing or another—for they were aware of how special and meaningful would have to be his niche in life for him to be happy there. But the circumstances, alas, happened to be far from normal: it was a time when young men were being drafted into the army. In school, he was safe from conscription.

Staying out of the army had naturally become the very first item in the young man's order of priorities. There was a war on, a beastly war, an evil war, a war in which no man of conscience could serve. It was criminal for the government to imperil the lives of *any* young men in such a war, but in his case it somehow seemed even more so.

As the years had worn on, the parents had found themselves agreeing with their son in most important things. True, they had struggled with him from time to time over the question of his appearance, but they did not, deep down, take that question very seriously. Slovenliness was after all a matter of general fashion among his peers, and like any fashion, would no doubt pass into oblivion of its own accord. Had it been necessary to do so, they would have struggled with him fiercely about whether it was valuable for him to have a college degree; but as things were, he would have his degree and would one day, they knew, be grateful for it. They sometimes thought his views about how both society and the people living in it ought to be transformed were a bit excessive. But they chalked his excesses up to his youth and his bitterness over the war. Fundamentally, they were very proud of him for being the sort of person who held such views. In everything that counted, then, they felt themselves to be at one with him.

About nothing, however, did they agree with him more unreservedly than about the subject of his going into the army. They were not principled pacifists. In their own youth there had been a war which they had supported with their whole beings; the father had himself served in that war, and while far from happy with the life of a soldier, had not suffered the least qualm of doubt that he was doing something good. But in the case of this particular war they shared their son's views wholeheartedly. It was a senseless bloodletting, based at best on an outmoded notion of the country's interest and at worst on the mere egomania of the country's President, and since it had no just cause, every single individual who fell in that war was as far as they were concerned the victim of plain murder. And beyond their staunch opposition to the government's Vietnam policy in general, there was the problem of their son in particular. Even in peacetime, it would have seemed to them quite out of the question that the boy be subjected to army life—a life so completely at odds with everything best in his temperament and feeling and upbringing. He was by nature totally unfitted for training in the arts of battle. He could no more learn to kill than he could fly. Not to mention the sheer brutality of the military ethos: how could so tender and spiritually open a creature survive in that world of brute, naked force? How could a child who had grown up with so delicately tuned a sense of right and so elegantly sensitive a system of human and social values be forced, now, to make his way, faceless and alone, in a jungle of ranking, bullying, and coercion? Their hearts ached merely for the fact that he had been confronted with such a possibility at all.

They were grateful at least that he had been allowed to seek protection in school. Yet the times were out of joint, for him no less than for the young men actually being marched off to war. He certainly did not feel grateful but rather raged at the thought that he and his friends and hundreds of thousands like them had been trapped between two unconditional alternatives; and while his parents did not at all share his views about his education, they sympathized with him. (Secretly they believed that had he not been forced to remain in school, he would have taken a different attitude toward it.) Even more than for his sense of entrapment, they pitied him for so shocking and brutal a discovery of the kind of evil that persisted in the world. He had been brought up to an altogether different vision of life from the one which greeted him daily in newspapers and on the television screen. Until this dirty business could be settled, young men like him—the very flower of mankind's best enlightenment on the meaning of social existence—were bound to remain fretful and disoriented. Nor could they as the boy's parents offer him any of the kind of wisdom and consolation they had once been able to bring when he was a child facing some strictly local cruelty. The world he now reviled, they had to confess, was a world

217

long accepted and acquiesced in by the members of their generation. About some things he had a wisdom far beyond their own.

So they were both shocked and not shocked when he announced to them a few days before his graduation from college that some people he knew had leased a farm where they were planning to retreat from society and live communally, subsisting on the labor of their own hands, and that he had made up his mind to join them. Everything among the members of the commune was to be shared equally—work, food, space, money—and each was to devote his life to a brotherly love and care for every other. They were shocked first of all because nothing in his upbringing, experience, or interest could ever remotely have connected him with the life of a farmer; the thought of him with his hands in the soil or wrapped around some tool or other was enough, even in the midst of the high emotion of the occasion, to bring laughter to their lips. They were shocked, second of all, because while they admired and to some extent shared his view that the drive for worldly success and goods emptied people's lives and deadened their souls, and while they had always recognized how serious a person he was, they had nevertheless looked forward to his pursuing a respectable and comfortable career. Retreating from the ruthlessness and crudity of the cash nexus, of society's worship of commercialism and its attendant corruption of the order of human worth, was something they themselves had always attempted to practice. But to retreat bodily this way from the world itself, and to create a way of life directly contradictory to the way this world has forever been organized was, it seemed to them, an attempt to make a startlingly literal truth out of a purely figurative vision.

On the other hand, if anyone could be expected to take

part in such an attempt, futile though they believed that attempt over the long haul to be, it would be their son. He knew no distinction—had never known a distinction—between thought and deed. They had been hearing for a few years now about young people banding together to form communes, making themselves into a kind of living embodiment of the principles of love and equality, of non-aggression and community. They ought to have known (perhaps, in talking it over later they agreed, they had really known) that their child was an obvious candidate for this sort of experiment.

The rules of the commune were simple, he told them. Everyone was to bring his relevant possessions and place them in the common pool. The work would be allotted on the basis of special skills or preferences, or failing that, by a system of rotation. They would grow food for themselves to eat and something extra to sell in order to keep themselves in incidentals, such as cigarettes, records, doctor bills, and so on. In a slow season, or should there be unforeseen expenses, they would take temporary jobs in a nearby town. One of their number—he was in fact the original organizer of the project—knew something about farming and had volunteered to teach the others. The farm had been leased in the name of one of the young man's good friends, who was collecting the earnings from a sizable trust fund left him by his grandparents, so they had a possible line of credit until they should be self-supporting. The "farmer" among them happened, along with his old lady, to be receiving a welfare stipend, and that, too, would be helpful.

Since they would have been willing to send him to graduate school if he had wanted to go, he said, he thought it would be all right for them to give him some of the money they would otherwise be spending. To begin with, there would be eight or nine on the commune, and before they got things organized, there might be something of a problem about supplying their table. None of the others was on good enough terms with his or her parents to ask for help.

At this last, the mother and father shuddered a little. The idea that there were contemporary parents, members of their own generation, so taken up with the issue of money that they would use it as a weapon of control over their children never failed to chill them. By all accounts, there were children roaming throughout the country, footloose and unprotected, children of middle-class parents (they supposed it was mostly lower-middle-class parents) so embittered by the disappointments and failures of their own lives that they would allow their children to sink or swim as they had once been forced to do. How could people like the mother and father in this situation not take at least one minute off from their anxiety over what their son was about to do to taste the pleasure of his serene confidence in them? If they had failed to make the world a sufficiently inviting place for him—as they clearly had; although given the state of the world, who could place the major burden of that failure on them?—they had in any case not driven him away from themselves, as so many others were evidently doing to their children.

They agreed on a sum to be their son's founding contribution to his community, amused by the innocence in him that made him think it would be enough to get along with. They did not mean to stint him but only to reinforce their unspoken hope that he would not long remain in his newfound life. There was also the draft. It no longer seemed likely that he would be called, but one could not tell about these things. They made him promise them, which was not all that difficult to do, that should there be even the faintest hint of a danger of his being drafted he would give up his plans and settle himself in graduate school.

And there was, in the end they had to face it, the possibility that these young people might truly be pointing the way for the future. Something was surely happening among the young these days—some higher demand from themselves and from life being made, some refusal to settle for or compromise with the way things were—that they were too sunk in the past to take any measure of. They had seen it in their son from almost the outset of his existence. Did they imagine that children could be fashioned from so utterly new a mold and there would be no lifelong, perhaps humanly transforming, consequences from it? They had to consider the question: was it really concern for their son's welfare, or was it only an unconscious fealty to the worship of money and status, that had dictated all their old, conventional ambitions for him?

In any case, as much as they might have thought they understood about their son's extraordinary selflessness, they found themselves overwhelmed that a boy who had grown up in the kind of ease and comfort he had grown up in should even be willing to undertake a life of such hardship as he had described to them. Perhaps, as their son had so long given them reason to suspect, they were after all standing at the brink of a new era.

The young man himself, of course, would never have uttered such a phrase as "new era." For if any one thing could have been said to characterize both his speech and his demeanor, it was a marked loathing for pomposity of any kind. However profound or far-reaching his thoughts, he spoke in a manner calculated to mark him the plainest and simplest of people. No polysyllabic would cross his lips where there was a monosyllabic to serve in its place; nor, if he could help it, would any term which had already acquired its resonance in the play of official public discussion. He also had a way of carrying himself, in a somewhat backward-leaning slouch, that signaled his apparent desire to create a living illustration of the old Biblical adage, "The last shall be first." Nevertheless, driving through the countryside to his new home—blanket, knapsack, skis, stereo equipment, and several cartons of record albums crammed into the back of his car—he was taken with the sensation of moving into some new field of human possibility.

A few of the members of his group, he knew, were seeking above all the clean air and physical well-being of a return to rural life. He was not. A few of them had quasireligious leanings toward the creation of a kind of Gandhian cottage-industry; one of the girls, for instance, was bringing a loom and intended to weave their cloth. He had no such leaning. He shared in their hatred of the city, but it was more abstract with him: he had come to despise the city as an institutionalized form of getting and spending, pushing and making way, winning and losing, rather than as literally a place of foul air and technology-poisoned food. He certainly respected the idea that one could cleanse one's soul in the primitive production of all one's daily needs, but this was not, privately, an idea that by itself truly impelled him. Once they had recovered their spirits a bit, his parents had teased him about becoming a farmer: he, who had never been nearer to the earth nor to the stuff which grows out of it than a few painfully dreary schoolboy afternoons of being dragged through botanical gardens; who had spent even his time in summer camp on the tennis courts, complaining bitterly when he was taken off them for a stroll in the woods; whose manual competence had extended no further than the hooking up of speakers to an amplifier. He had made no effort to explain to them that his own particular interest in or capacity for mastering the arts of farming, that farming itself, was utterly beside the point. His journey to the commune was not a journey to a farm—though he imagined that that part of things would one way and another take care of itself—not even, strictly speaking, a journey away from the corruptions of the city; it was a journey toward the two things people have always wanted and had never before found the real means of achieving: namely, love and freedom. In that farmhouse, with his fellow communitarians, he was about to find the realization of the only genuinely saving human ideals.

Love and freedom were forms of the social relation upon which the highest accolades had been bestowed by everyone he had ever known and everything he had read and heard in the course of his entire life. They had been honored, however, as had most other ideals in a relentlessly materialist civilization, largely in the breach. For the secret of true love was that it was a relation which could obtain only in a condition of equality; it was nothing less than a full and honest and open acceptance of one another without extraneous demands, without conditions, without any elements of subordination and superordination. The model of love which had had the greatest influence over the traditional definition of the term, that is, the love between parent and child, had been a snare and a delusion, trapping people into habits of obedience and tyranny that had extended beyond the family into the whole of society. This relation of authority and dependency, traditionally deemed by mankind of all relations to be worthiest of the very name of love, had served as the model for many of society's most flagrant enactments of tyranny: boss and worker, government and people, black and white, husband and wife. The love of and for one's fellows, growing out of a situation in which there was no such thing as rank or distinction or ascription of roles, he visualized as a kind of "revolution backward into being." (He had read the phrase once—he could not remember where—and it had seemed to him the perfect name for his desire.) To give this love or to receive it, to find one's most essential human support and sympathy, one had to accomplish nothing—one only had to exist.

And the secret of true freedom was that it was a relation which could obtain only in a condition of mere subsistence, of living without reference to money; for freedom was nothing less than the possibility of being oneself and only oneself, without handing over one's spirit as a hostage to some future promise of wealth or security. As with love, the traditionally defining model of freedom was a travesty of the very thing it presumed to bespeak. The so-called free man, granted just as much political liberty as was needed to make him a voluntary partner to the endless, mindless production of riches, was the very picture of enslavement. He was allowed to move about with the appearance of being unhampered only so that he might more effectively do exactly as society had decreed for him to do. The goods with which he surrounded himself he had been brainwashed to need and desire; the economic security he was so grateful to be allowed to procure for himself and his family was no more than the bait with which his oppressors had long laid their trap for him. If he was a decent man, he might pity the empty-handed—more likely, he condemned them—without realizing that it was they who had succeeded in escaping the terrible burden of obligation which was meant to keep a man's life in chains. What else after all was a career, a "beautiful" home, a plan for retirement, an insurance policy? Thus, the possibility of existing almost literally from hand to mouth the young man also visualized as a kind of revolution. To refuse the beguilements of wealth and status was to live unentangled, of and in and for oneself, pushing no one, being pushed by no one, at peace with one's desires and therefore with the desires of others—in other words, to live as a truly free man.

It was in the nature of both their enterprise and their feelings about it that he and his group should have little impulse to proselytize others. Love and freedom as they understood these terms pulled in precisely the opposite direction from zealotry—indeed, it was fundamental to the principles of the commune that its members should account themselves the kind of people who aspired only to live. This was another reason why he could never have dreamed of making so thunderous a proclamation as that he was the harbinger of a new era. Still and all, he was quietly convinced that his new commune, in concert with all the other communes like it, would in the long run have a decisive effect on American society.

There were members of his generation—some of them were friends and former close associates of his—who were calling for an actual armed revolution. They demanded the destruction of capitalism, dreamed of fomenting a massive insurrection in the armed forces, of opening the prisons, of taking over the universities in which they were being forced to serve time, of destroying the power of the police. They spoke salaciously of the time when blood might flow in the streets. They marched under a variety of flags—some of these actually the emblems of foreign powers—pledged their loyalty to this or that specific body of revolutionary doctrine, and worked feverishly to organize disciplined cadres of the faithful. He felt no stirring op-

position to these revolutionaries—he was after all connected to them by the bond of their common refusal to countenance the prevailing sick and rotten values of society—but
they had failed to ignite the least spark of real interest or
commitment on his part. Their way was not his way; he
had neither a personal taste for it nor faith in it. They
wished to do, to act, to deal in categories of power. He
wished only to be himself. They used the language of violence and claimed to be preparing themselves for violence.
He could think of nothing which by his lights would make
the risk of violence seem justified. Perhaps the recourse to
force and terror was justified—he could see many of the
arguments—but not for him.

In any case, he could think of no form of resistance so
effective, so unanswerable, as that of passive resistance.
This was not exactly a matter of doctrine, but rather more
a translation of his private experience. Even as a small
child, he had discovered that there was no way for those in
authority to make him do what he simply and quietly refused to do. They might try to persuade him, to bribe him,
even to blackmail him, but as long as he remained impervious to any of these efforts, there was nothing further they
could do. Imagine such a discovery acted upon en masse.
If every young man in America of eligible age, for instance, had in the same immovable and quiet fashion simply not shown up to register for the draft, the entire history of the world might have been ineradicably altered.

The blood which according to his revolutionary friends
was one day to flow in the streets, if it did—and while he
was willing to make conversation with them about it, he
could not actually imagine or believe that it would—was as
likely to be revolutionary blood as capitalist blood. Aside
from his revulsion at bloodshed, he could not see, then,
what would be the purpose of such a conflagration. But
the commune, or any similar declaration of nonparticipa-

tion in the system, could truly turn things over. For once people caught sight of the possibility of being loved without first submitting to authority, once they were forced to contemplate the vision of freedom that inheres in a life of being without doing, of thought and feeling untrammeled by the discipline and self-denial of the great race for wealth, the very fabric of their existence would be rent forever. They might rage for a time with envy and spite, as his parents had over his liberation from the imprisonment of attending to his personal appearance, but in the end their deathly habits of obedience and futile calculation for the future would be undermined beyond reinforcement.

Already he had seen in his parents' eyes, particularly his father's, as they bade him good-bye a certain ill-concealed look of fear and admiration . . . and envy, envy, envy. He did not expect that they would now throw up everything and rush off to a life of self-subsistence, but at least he could imagine that something in the certainty of their assumptions about what was the good and proper and rewarding way to live had forever turned sour.

His settlement in the large and shabby house belonging to their new property was thus accomplished in a mood of high hope. The farm had been leased from an old man who could no longer profitably run it alone and had escaped with his meager capital in the form of savings to warm his weary bones in Florida. The old man had left them a few sticks of furniture, a kitchen table, some iron bedsteads and mattresses, a couple of chests of drawers, an unsprung sofa. The weather being warm, they left every window they were able to budge open for three days to let in the earth-scented air and spent several pleasurable hours sitting in the meadow, passing around sprucely rolled cigarettes of marijuana and discussing plans for how to make the place habitable.

In the course of one particularly giddy session, they took

to rolling about in the unmown weeds, then splashing one another with the muddy water of a little cow pond, finally to dousing one another with great handfuls of mud. They could not stand up to return to the house for their laughter. In his mind's eye, the young man could see the faces of middle-class America looking on, aghast and stricken with the recognition that life as they had lived it had been a waste.

His stereo, being the best of those possessed by the group, was given place of honor in the main parlor. His skis were stowed in the barn. And within the space of a couple of days, he and one of the young women in the group had arrived at an agreement to share a bedroom.

He could almost physically feel himself uncoiling from the pressures of the past few years—school, the draft, the anxiety of his parents about what was to become of him; even he had not known how great those pressures had been.

Not that there were not tensions in his new community. Some of these were almost immediately apparent. Two of the young women, for instance, had undertaken to do the cooking. "Undertaken" was not quite the right word because no one had actually asked them. But they had very strong convictions on the subject of eating, how it was related to everything in life, not only bodily health but temperament, intelligence, mood, and spiritual setting; it was vitally important to them that the commune should eat the right food prepared in the proper way. And he did not much care for the meals that resulted from such philosophy. They were composed largely of grain and fruits and vegetables and honey. There were odd concoctions— much touted for their salubrious properties by their authors, who had been required to spend hours over them— made up of wild leaves and grasses discovered growing alongside the road to the nearby village. In the first couple of weeks he had found numerous pretexts for going to the village and each time had headed straight for the general store where he stood at the back and wolfed down two or three candy bars, feeling dreadfully guilty. Finally he knew that the only way to make a peaceable settlement with the problem was simply to suppress all natural interest in the pleasures of the palate. Moreover, the cooks themselves had begun to grumble and one night, no longer able to contain themselves, had burst upon the group with the loud complaint that after having completed the chore of preparing the meals, they had also been left to put the kitchen back in order. This complaint was apparently settled by a general agreement to include kitchen cleanup in the roster of rotating duties. That, however, also proved to be unsatisfactory because when the task fell to certain of the male members of the group—most notable among them the young man himself—the job was not done with sufficient care and had to be redone the next day.

It was too late in the year to attempt much more than cutting down the fields for the next spring's planting. Here again the bulk of the task fell to the man who had taken it upon himself to be the commune's agricultural expert. Everyone was assigned some share in the mowing. A couple of people claimed to find the work rather soothing and enjoyable for an hour or two a day. The others found it quite tedious and invented certain small diversions— hayfights, for instance—in order to keep themselves mindful of the joys and glories of their new life. In the end, at the suggestion of the one whose income it was that for the time being was keeping them going, they hired a neighboring farmer to come in with his tractor for a few days. But before they had hit upon this expedient, the expert had grown ever so slightly irascible about getting them all down to serious work. The young man had not liked the tone in his voice that week. It carried, he thought, something of the melody of that will to subordinate, to be the acknowledged leader in a race for power, which the commune had been created precisely to eradicate. The man had after all *chosen* to be responsible for the group's efforts at farming. Others had made a different choice. Who was he to set his choice above theirs? The habits of the world Out There would clearly take a certain time to die among individuals less conscious and certain than the young idealist of their moral purpose.

Very quickly, two schools of thought developed about what to do with the house. One party recommended that they spend the slow winter months ahead in painting the place and fixing it up. There was a good deal of beautiful old furniture lying about in attics in a farming district like this one; they could pick it up for a song and restore it. The other party favored leaving the house as it was, a symbol of the group's determination to live without the intrusion of any bourgeois frivolities. As for painting, these latter would be willing to do only so much as was needed to keep the place from rotting at the seams. The discussions on this point became rather acrimonious, the would-be decorators taking umbrage at the association of their wish to create an agreeable environment with mere middle-class convention. In the end it was settled, again by the man who was footing most of their bills, that a limited amount of shopping for amenities would be undertaken, but no more than would be enhancing to their physical comfort. The young man, who had no very strong feelings on either side, though he had looked with pleasure on the prospect of painting and mixing colors, was nevertheless disquieted by the weight that was being given to money, and particularly to the man who was dispensing the money, in so many of their deliberations. He and his girl discussed this several times in the privacy of their bedroom and came to the conclusion that in all future decisions of the group the man with the money should be given the least, not the most, attention, for his views were likely to be tainted. And he, and they, clearly needed the discipline of drawing their conclusions without reference to the old bugaboo of finance.

Such tensions, however, were inevitable. The human spirit, he was not such a child as not to know, was a substance that could hardly be reshaped overnight. They had on the whole been doing very well. It wanted a bit more experience, and beyond experience, a process of learning to deal openly and honestly with everyone's leftover private difficulties, before they could live together as the absolute equals of their ideal vision.

As the cold weather set in, and they were drawn more and more to the comforts of long indoor afternoons around the stereo set, they ventured far into the intimacy that would finally seal their cohesion as a new and true family. They spoke of themselves and of one another, of their respective pasts, of their present pain and pleasure, of their ideas and of their feelings—passing from lips to lips the pipe filled with marijuana that was both the goad to, and totem of, their brotherhood. Their talk was unorganized and seemingly aimless—the final and most significant throwing off of the lonely privacy that lay at the heart of the ethic of selfish acquisition and property.

But by no one's express intention, these conversations began to take on a ritual aspect, a sort of prescribed and predictable back-and-forth that gave hint of a focused purpose. One of the members of the group would be reminded by something in the afternoon of a past experience, and the others would be prompted by his narrative to launch upon a gentle, loving, but instructive analysis of his character. From there they would somehow, imperceptibly but inevitably, move on to the subject of his relation to the group, his particular role therein, and especially the emotional difficulties he was having with that role. Sometimes there would be anger; sometimes, particularly if the elected center of these attentions happened to be one of the young women, there would be tears; but everyone agreed that talk of this kind was vitally important, indeed essential, to both the quality and survival of their community. In fact, it was what they had come to this place for. After all, anyone could become a farmer. Anyone could, if he were forced to, provide with his own two hands the basic necessities of life. Only bona fide pioneers on the frontier of a new order of human relations could brave the possibility of living together honestly, without the shelter of social pretenses.

The young man had enjoyed these sessions enormously at first. Once or twice he had actually felt a great lump of love come into his throat, so that he dared not speak lest he, too, like the young woman into whose hang-up with her mother he had just had a blazing insight, were to burst into tears. He had much to say to his newfound brothers and sisters, so much that sometimes he was aware of a flood of words tumbling from his lips in no controllable order. But after the first rush of unburdening himself, he began to notice certain disparities and inequities in the group's conduct. His turn to be laid bare seemed to come around less often than those of others. Two or three people were subtly managing, by laying unspoken claim to problems and neurotic sensitivities greater than those of the rest of the group, to preempt the major part of their attentions. To tell the truth he soon wearied of the stories of these self-appointed special cases, which were basically the same two or three stories told over and over with an apparently endless supply of minor variations, and he felt the stirrings of resentment at the unremitting demand for his sympathetic involvement. Moreover, on those few occasions when the group did appear to be willing to concern itself with him, he thought he detected a certain uncalled-for abruptness in their comments, a certain lack of sensitivity in the response to what he said, a certain implicit urging that he get done and move offstage.

By Christmastime, he and his girl were quarreling badly, at first exchanging tight-lipped, whispered reproaches behind closed doors and finally shouting at each other, stamping up and down in the cold, out behind the barn. She had acquired a peculiar habit of speaking of and to him contemptuously, even sneeringly, in the presence of the others. In the course of one particularly edgy circle-jerk (as he and she had come in private to call the daily sessions of the group), she had betrayed a confidence of their bed. He had never before in his life known the kind of violence she could inspire in him. When he had called her a cruel, selfish, murdering bitch, she had countered by heaping upon his head a veritable avalanche of scorn for being, as she put it, "a cowardly shit-eater." He had never once, she told him, defended her against the snide and nasty treatment she was forced to put up with every single day from the other girls in the house. He had come to her for comforting with every hurt, real or imagined, down to the tiniest splinter in his toe; and yet he had looked on passively while this one had hassled her, that one had spread ugly stories about her, and the other one had contrived to stick her with dirty jobs it was not her turn to do. To become the patsy, the good little slavey, of some mama's boy brought up to believe he must not lift a finger for any female, she could have stayed at home. He was like all the others, the ones she had come here to get away from, regarding her as just another sexual dumping-ground.

His father had sent him a check for Christmas. One morning he hooked his skis onto the car and in a thrill of guilt and defiance, cashed the check for himself and took off for a holiday at a nearby ski resort. He would of course return, but by the time he did, less notice would be taken of his request to move into another room.

As it was to happen, his girl was to leave the commune soon after anyway, spending a long mysterious afternoon in the village making phone calls and being whisked away the following afternoon in a battered old car that had been dispatched to call for her. She barely said good-bye.

In late March or early April the group intended to do their planting. After the depressing blow of their first defection, a wave of high humor returned to the household with the arrival of seed catalogues and talk of the coming summer and autumn, when they would be dining gloriously on their own corn and tomatoes. Even the household cooks softened the Savonarola edges of their pronunciation of the word "nutriments." There was one small but contained battle over the issue of whether or not to use chemical fertilizer, but at the contemplation of how much work there was to be done, the general inclination was to abide by the judgment of their agricultural expert.

Who was once more, the young man noted, coming into his own. A further mental note was made to stay out of the fields. He had already had a sufficient foretaste of what could become of equality and brotherhood, even in a commune, under conditions where one man arrogated unto himself some special responsibility or expertise. So he set up a makeshift easel in a little-used back parlor, got himself some supplies, and set about busying himself with painting. He painted several rather gaudy abstractions which were actually, it amused him to know, scenes of mass sexual congress and a series of depictions of death stalking the battlefield.

There were many other signs, besides the growing swagger of the self-styled expert, that things could never be quite as promised in this community. A certain acerbity had entered into their relations. Intimacy had not made them tenderer or freer with one another, but on the contrary had pushed them into assuming ever more rigid roles. They were like a cast of characters, and no one ever seemed to be out of the character first assigned to him. The women had grown restive and touchy, watchful about a whole range of trivial issues of male-female manners and status. They refused duty in the kitchen and laundry. One of them marched into his parlor-studio one morning and announced that if he was an artist, she was an artist, too; and proceeded in every way she knew how to make the day unpleasant for him.

He did not feel well, either. During that winter all of them had come down with some kind of flu that made their bones ache and left them feeling debilitated for weeks. They were given a variety of herbal brews by the superintendents of the group's health—now quite enlivened at the prospect of so massive an opportunity to minister to the ailing—and endless lectures on the evils of antibiotics. Eventually he stopped aching but never seemed to enjoy a complete recovery. He found himself considerably irritated by the sight of his fellow communitarians shuffling about with pallid faces and runny eyes. Their struggles with ill health only seemed to underline his growing impression that they were all desperately preoccupied with themselves.

By the time it was announced that they were ready to begin plowing, he was spending most of his time in hiding, shut up in his room with a book or buried behind his easel. He made one effort to join the group at work, breaking his resolution not to put himself at the mercy of their games of power. The sun was shining, and he was drawn by the loud voices and laughter he could hear through his window: the voices and laughter held out the promise that things would once more be the way they were in those first glorious weeks when they had rolled around in the grass easing the constriction and phony purposefulness of the city. He should have known better. He did, of course, know better. But resolutely hopeful naïf that he was, he could not even yet quite abandon the ideals that had brought him here.

There was no doubt about it, his comrades were out that day to do him down. The agriculturist had become no more than a mere work boss, barking orders, making decisions, instructing everybody about what they were to do, growing impatient with those who appeared to be lagging, raising his voice, shunting them all about. He appeared to be not altogether certain of how to proceed, and this uncertainty, instead of humbling him and making him amenable to the decisions of others, led him to drive them even harder. The young man had often in his childhood heard his father speak of a certain executive in his office—the man to whom he himself was at that time, as they say in bureaucratic circles, "reporting"—who was unfit either by skill or intelligence to be directing the work of his subordinates. The man had clearly reached his eminence by sheer politicking or perhaps even through blackmail. His father had raved, had sometimes required three or four martinis to compose himself for dinner, had once been diagnosed by a doctor as "pre-ulcerous," all because he had been forced to accept as a boss this idiotic man who was entitled

236

to his role by nothing more than his success at having manipulated the system. Then, finally his father had moved up to a position of peerdom with his former superior. The young man was suddenly reminded of his father's stories as he watched his comrade struggling, face and shirt dripping with sweat, to deal with some possibly broken connection on the tractor they had leased. He himself, he was aware, could not have dealt with the tractor at all, but then he made no pretense at being able to. He began to suspect that the reason the group had been persuaded to take up farming in the first place was that they had been manipulated into doing so by someone just looking for a cheap shot at leadership. The talk about liberating oneself by subsisting only on the fruits of the labor of one's own hands had merely been a front for dragging them all into a trap where one of them could play king and the others play his loyal and dependent servitors. They had managed through the winter without this self-appointed dictator, buying their groceries in a grocery store; no doubt it was only because they were a bunch of blind sheep that they were being led into the pasture like this now that spring had come.

They were certainly an altered group from the one that had cavorted in the outdoors less than a year ago—altered perhaps most of all, he could not help feeling, bitterly, in their relations with him. For not only was the "boss" expressing annoyance with the inadequacy of his efforts, the whole group appeared to be following the leader and presuming to remark upon the young man's clumsiness, his failure to pull his fair share of the collective weight, the sloppiness of his results. He had volunteered for this work, he ultimately reminded them, or had they forgotten that they had come here originally to learn how to be free men? *They* might have so far lost sight of their ideals as to be willing to create a miniature of the system—a little replica of all the pushing around and being pushed around, all the putting of shoulders to the wheels of other men's convenience, that conditioned people for service in the army of the Protestant ethic—but he for one had not. He returned to the house with aching back and scraped knuckles, ruing the impulse that had brought him out and anguished for the way his former friends were being contaminated by the same trivial morality they had once set out so bravely to destroy.

He was for a while to think of this particular day as the occasion of his first serious break with the group, but later he was to understand that his disaffection had taken hold some time before. During his brief holiday, when he had run off to go skiing, he had experienced the kind of sense of well-being he had not known for years. The world, the war, the group, were far away. Coming down the slopes, he knew what it felt like to be a free man. At the top, there had been the prospect of the satisfying descent ahead, and at the bottom was waiting no other burden, of action or of feeling, than the need to get up to the top again. He felt as gentle as the snow squeaking beneath his skis, and his heart was filled with love. He had stayed on until he had only enough money left for the gas to return home.

Some days after he had stormed back to the house from the fields he made one last-ditch effort to turn the group aside from its growing entrapment in the worldly order. While they were gathered at dinner, he proposed that they rethink their plan to become actual farmers. Planting was scheduled to begin any time now, and it would soon be too late for them to step back and consider what they were doing to themselves. He filled the pipe with marijuana, passed it around, and delivered a speech in which he painted for them the picture of the life they had set out here to find: a life lived in so pure, so insistent an igno-rance of the trivia of getting and spending that they might become a kind of band of holy fools who could overturn the world. The visions, the passions, the pleasures of the flesh vouchsafed to them through the long winter nights by the generous application of LSD would be as nothing compared with what they might achieve simply rising from their beds each morning. Once the world had seen such an example of human felicity, how could any manmade sys-tem for the oppression and exploitation of individuals stand against it? Men might walk off their jobs, shutting down the whole ugly soul-killing process of production, restoring the countryside to its beauty and humankind to its natural birthright. Women might desist from their end-less slavish round—at this, one of the females at the table snorted—of acquisition and consumption, freeing them-selves and their husbands and children for a life of love and play. Children would grow up savoring the very blood that coursed through their veins.

Instead, he continued, they were opting for a life that would be nasty, brutish, and short—no less nasty, brutish, and short than the lives of any people organized into a community of production, with its overseers and under-lings, leaders and led, its saving and scraping and planning and putting-off, its sacrifice of equality and the concern of every being for every other to the great chimera of securi-ty. There was to be a baby born in the commune in early autumn. A new generation. Did they not owe it to this baby to make something better of its community than a dingy, dreary version of the community they themselves had grown up in? Over the past several months they had talked for hours and hours and hours about their parents, about the pinched spirits and mean intentions of middle-class people who had sold themselves into the slavery of householding and job-holding and worry for the future. Was not the same thing happening to them now, and would not the nervous system of their own new generation be branded with the same repression and anxiety? Of course, the baby would at least be growing up without being "owned" by its parents, as they all had once been, but of what use would be the attachment to a whole body of surrogate parents if one's extended family were all equally busily engaged in grooming one for a future of aspiring toward the standard assortment of mean and narrow little goals?

He could sense as he was speaking that some of the members of the group were being swayed by him. The smoke from the pipe was bringing back the old familiar odor of softening affection, eyes had grown wide, and the long-absent talk of dreams and ideals was warming some of the icy chill that had set in to a number of eager laboring-men's spines.

The mood was broken, however, when the man with the trust fund—the inevitable one, the young man told himself later, the daddy, the one who pays the bills—raised the question of how they would eat and meet the rent. He had been carrying them for nearly a year now, the man said; his bank account, one check from the young man's father, and a few welfare payments—stopped after a statewide investigation of welfare fraud—had put the food into all their mouths and kept a roof over all their heads (the young man laughed silently to himself at the way the issue of money always and inevitably bred the same rhetoric of food and shelter). He was willing to carry them further, had not dreamed of withdrawing his support or even keeping books about who was contributing how much. But he was after all not going to be some mere moneybags they had all got their hooks into. For his part, that was not *his*

240

ideal of equality. He had helped to organize the commune—in fact, you could say it was mainly his idea—because he longed to cleanse himself of the taint of his family fortune, to put it to use in the creation of some common benefit. And he had more than once, he would now freely confess, gotten the feeling that he was being used. To cite only one example, it was his money which had been paid out in the purchase of canvas and paints so that a certain commune member could enjoy the fiction that he was some kind of artist; but that same commune member had somehow mysteriously found the means, when his old lady was giving him a bad time, to rush off in the car he had contributed to the group—but was once more clearly claiming for his own—and have himself a high old time on the ski slopes. He would not call that community or brotherhood. He would call that being played for a sucker. So now he wanted to know: was this group or was this group not aiming to live by the sweat of its own brow and to eat of the fruit of its own land and all that other stuff about which so many pretty speeches had been made? Or did they expect him merely to go on playing Big Daddy?

Thus diverted from the young man's visions and exhortations, the group proceeded to embark upon a discussion of just what each of them had done, had meant to do, had not meant to do, had fallen short of doing, or had succeeded in doing, for every other. The discussion went on far into the night. Never, they all agreed, had they attained to such heights of sincerity.

The young man himself took no part in this discussion, since at the conclusion of the attack upon him he had simply stood up and left the room. All night he lay on his bed seething, tossing from side to side, muttering, now and then weeping tears of rage. He felt as if he had been playing his best and hardest at a game whose rules had been

241

changed in the middle without his having been told. Talk about having been taken! He tried to apply his mother's old suggestion, and imagine that the man with the money was more unhappy, more to be pitied, at this moment than he, but that only made him angry with his mother. The truth was—he had been working his way toward it for months but had till now kept turning it aside for the sake of his daily comfort and convenience—the truth was, that neither the commune nor the revolution it was supposed to be setting an example for would ever eradicate the power of wealth and ownership. These, he now knew, had been too deeply graven into the human psyche. His own pure-hearted refusal to stand watch over the boundaries of possession, to preserve the sanctity of what belonged to him and what to another, had brought him no freedom from the age-old need to compete for the rights of territory; it had brought him instead a . . . kick in the ass. To which latter he was now prepared to add a reflexive kick of his own for having failed so badly to understand the nature of his true position, first within this little community and from there, within the world at large. Freedom and love, freedom and love—these he had experienced only, and at their highest intensity, while sweeping downhill on his skis. There was a message to him in this, a message he would have once and for all to decipher if he were every truly to become the master of his soul.

Two days later he set out from the commune, having reclaimed his car, his skis, and his stereo. His paintings he left behind as a legacy to the group. He stopped off at home only long enough to collect some money and some camping equipment, and set off for a few weeks on a cross-country drive. He needed to look at the world again and to complete that first hesitant reassessment of his predicament. He drove to California and back, and by the time he returned, he had found the resolution he was seeking.

His parents, who had been too rushed by his sudden arrival from the commune and departure for his journey to express much more than a certain benign bewilderment over this new turn of events, were able by the day of his return to greet him with proper enthusiasm. Though they had offered little firm objection at the time, they had actually been quite unhappy with his decision to become a commune member. They had understood very well what he was seeking, they had told him, but had subsequently spent many nights in a state of sleepless worry about the way he had taken to find it. They were delighted—though, he noticed, they were also, at the edges, a touch fearful— to have him back. His mother burned most of his clothes, claiming they would not even serve her as dusting rags.

He knew that the decision he had taken on his trip would please them, for he had decided to return to school. As soon as it was feasible to do so, he would make application to law school. There were a few preliminary courses he needed to take, and while he made up his requirements, he would look around for a suitable school to apply to. Unaccountably—they at least would have found it unaccountable—the thought of their pleasure over all this made him furious. They were bound to regard his new resolution as a kind of victory for their side, that is, for the side of all those who were content to pull themselves together neatly and offer up their lives to the system. It became critically important to him to make them understand and feel that his decision represented no victory for the kind of things they stood for. He had if anything less intention than ever before to step into his father's shoes.

He put off telling them of his plans for as long as possible. And then one night, because the school year was almost upon him, because they had so virtuously and so judiciously and so painfully refrained from asking him what was to come next, and because he needed their help, he laid before them his new vision of the future. As he spoke, he felt the urgency of his need to snuff out any stray spark of smugness of self-satisfaction that his words might be kindling in their hearts.

There was no decent way for a man to live within the system, he told them—no way to remain kind, sensitive, spiritually sound, at peace with oneself if one allowed "them" to own one's soul. In order to avoid this, he had taken so extreme a measure as going off to become a communitarian farmer. That measure had not worked. For the problem was not so much to take the boy out of the system as to take the system out of the boy, and he had discovered that even in so radically reorganized a community as he and his erstwhile friends had attempted to create, one did not necessarily escape the false values of the world around. A man could only be free to live as his own natural spirit and instinct told him, he now recognized, on his own. He was going to law school not in order to become a better-tooled cog in the great social machine, as it would clearly give his parents so much joy to imagine, but because training in the law would offer him the widest possibility to use the system for his own purposes. With a law degree in hand, he would find himself a good spot in some firm or corporation, pull down his forty or fifty thousand a year (at this his father started a little, opened his mouth as if to speak, but remained silent), and reserve the living kernel of himself to himself and for himself. The true revolution, he now saw, lay in taking hold of whatever benefits the system had to offer and secretly giving nothing of one's own substance in return. That way society could be made to be beneficent against its own knowledge or will. Any other method of capturing society's beneficence, or trying to force it, was childish.

Later, in a private conversation with his father, he spoke more of this matter. The men of his father's generation, he said, were little more than slaves, however well paid or well rewarded. For they had put not only their hands but their hearts and minds, their very private selves, at the service of their bosses or businesses. They not only worked as they were told to do, but thought as they were told to do and lived as they were told to do, only in order that they might work harder. Their notions of social and personal obligation, their standards and morals, their family lives, their pleasures, their desires, had all been dictated to them by a system whose real purpose was to keep them obediently and gratefully in harness until they got too old to be of any productive use. Whence it cast them out, grateful still, with a few junky baubles to their name and the illusion that they had enjoyed a life well and honorably spent. And in the meantime, they had been tricked into lending their best and most earnest efforts to such noble efforts as plundering the land, murdering the young, and ripping off the innocent.

In a way, he conceded, it was not altogether their fault. (After all, he told himself, he was not the sort of mean and brutal person who could not sympathize with another's experience.) He himself had learned how powerful was the sway of conformity to the common ethic. How much more powerful that sway must be over ordinary people who had never found the means to attack the system at its very first premise, namely, that what the majority of one's fellows felt and cared about and believed must be right. Thus, those like his father, who were now in middle age, had been swindled into imagining that they were fortunate be-

245

cause they had been able to give their family nice houses and good food and the petty extra comforts they could buy with their hard-earned, their desperately hard-earned, life-sacrificing money. Whereas things like nice houses and good food and everyday comforts should not be seen as a species of good fortune but only as the minimal proper due of every single human at birth. One should not be grateful for them, one should regard them as the very least that one might expect out of life.

If he, for example, thought for one moment that he might end up living as his father had—working like a dog and spending his substance, giving up most of life's genuinely warm pleasures, taking for himself only a pittance of the wealth he was adding to the system, and proud of nothing more than having acquitted an obligation handsomely to support a wife and children—if he thought that he would one day be forced to sum up his own life in such terms, he would slit his throat then and there. He for one was never going to be grateful for so small a favor. He had rather better things in mind than that. Law school was not going to signify his surrender to any thin and paltry necessity; for him it would be a means only, a means precisely for living beyond the reach of necessity.

The father was naturally somewhat upset by this conversation. It had never occurred to him that he might one day stand accused in this particular way. The description of his life stung him at first as a grave injustice, and defenses, denials, justifications rushed to his lips. The ideas and attitudes his son had charged him with holding—accurately characterized, he would agree, for most people—had not been his ideas and attitudes at all. Nor had it been in his own home that the young man had witnessed the kind of dreary accommodation to things of which he complained. On the contrary, it might somewhere along the line have come to the boy's attention that the thirsting after higher things for which he so highly regarded himself was more likely a product of his upbringing than anything else. How many other young men did he imagine ran off to communes with the fervent prayers, albeit also the doubts and misgivings, of his father and mother?

Still, as he continued to listen, the father's agitation gave way to a kind of deep and quiet melancholy. If the boy's tone and emphasis seemed needlessly harsh, much of what he said was nevertheless true. How sadly true, indeed, he himself had grown ever more aware in the past few years. He was, to be sure, though it never failed to startle him to hear the term being applied to himself, middle-aged. He had by now spent the vast proportion of the total of his waking hours in one way or another on the disciplines of his job, and the vast proportion of his inner life either stoking or attempting to bank the fires of his ambition. And what, the question had lately come to haunt him, could he really say he had to show for it? A lovely wife, a lovely home, and lovely children, he would answer in a tone that always echoed through his head as a mockery of the accents of *his* parents' generation; also two cars, a house at the beach, an annual trip to Europe, a carpeted office, a goodly quantity of the envy of his uncarpeted colleagues and one-car neighbors, a fat life-insurance policy, and enough both of power and responsibility to make likely that his wife would not too many years from now collect on it. He *had* done what he was told all his life; he *had* been granted what had to be seen as only a derisory return— handsome as it might once have looked to him—on the amount of wealth he had produced for others; and like a beaten, timid old retainer, he *had*, at least until recently, been grateful for it.

But how much play, how much laughter, how much simple physical health, had it cost him? When his son had mentioned "life's genuinely warm pleasures," he could feel the flush rising to his cheeks. For such thoughts, too, had been prominent in his own reckonings. He felt as if the boy must at some time or other have been reading his mind. What of all the sweets he had denied himself to avoid the danger of being deflected from his appointed course—young girls not taken, interests not pursued, flights of escape canceled—and which he would now go to his grave without having tasted? The evenings of self-conscious overage highjinks that he and his wife and many of his friends and their wives now and then indulged in, feasts of pot and pornographic movies and once even a timid little fiasco of an orgy, were no substitute for a life of love and freedom such as his son was now daring to make for himself.

The father did not throw himself to the floor or into his son's arms. He sat silent in his chair, unmoving, face fixed into what he hoped was a dignified and maybe even masterfully inscrutable expression. He said no more than that, of course, the young man could count on them in every possible way to see him through his schooling. He had no wish to discuss the old familiar feelings that his son had once more freshly roused in him—not so much for the boy's sake as for his own. He recognized the clutching sensation at the pit of his stomach and knew that it would be with him now for a whole day or two if he gave in too far to his emotions.

Afterward, the young man was under the impression that he had not been able to reach his father, that his ideas had made no dent in that great thick wall of conventional piety behind which the old man had always kept himself hidden and protected. And since the old man had absolutely refused to understand him, he shooed away all remaining pangs of guilt for having talked so brutally of his father's failed and wasted life.